T0243965

The question, "Are we experiencing a racial divide?" is easy to answer. How to heal this divide is a conversation we should all be interested in right now. Derwin pastors each of us with his words as he shows us why this all matters and what God's Word says about it all. With every word of this book, I felt pastored, encouraged, and enlightened.

JAMIE IVEY, bestselling author and host of *The Happy Hour with Jamie Ivey* podcast

When I want to learn about healing, I listen to someone who has been a healer. That's one of the many reasons I listen to Derwin Gray. He has not just advocated for racial justice and reconciliation, he has worked toward it and demonstrated it in his life and ministry.

ED STETZER, executive director of the Billy Graham Center at Wheaton College

Derwin Gray is a trusted voice for looking at what the Bible has to say about one of the most divisive topics of our day. In *How to Heal Our Racial Divide* Dr. Gray sets us up by looking into both the narrative arc of Scripture as well as its explicit commands (orthodoxy) and then moves us to the application of the Scriptures in our disciple-making (orthopraxy). There are many books on this subject but few that deal with it as biblically and hopefully as this one.

MATT CHANDLER, lead pastor of The Village Church

America's racism is not so much its original sin as it is the church's scourge. In this book Derwin Gray, block by block, slowly and carefully, lays the foundations and begins to build the Bible's own house designed by God for all people. Racism's scourge has always had a biblical prophetic word (sin) and a biblical prophetic vision (the multiethnic church), but many have walked away from God's design.

We need fewer people criticizing and more pastors like Derwin Gray creating solutions to the problem. This book can help heal our nation. Be Tov!

SCOT McKNIGHT, professor of New Testament at Northern Seminary

This book is an inspiring and timely grace-driven manifesto from one of the world's most respected preachers. Avoiding both simplistic answers and despairing cynicism, this book shows us why racial justice and reconciliation are not distractions from the gospel but a central theme of Jesus' call to repentance and life together. Read this book and pass it along to a friend. We need it right now.

RUSSELL MOORE, public theologian at *Christianity Today*

Dr. Derwin Gray is not an author with a big social media following that he leverages to talk about things he's not personally invested in. Derwin is all in on God's multiethnic family in every sphere of his life. *How to Heal Our Racial Divide* is a hopeful offering which pours out of a life committed to healing the divide.

DR. BRYAN LORITTS, author of *Insider Outsider* and teaching pastor at The Summit Church

Why are you always talking about racism? Just preach the gospel! Derwin Gray says he hears this a lot—so do I. I love Gray's answer: because it's a part of the world's story of sin, because it was on Jesus' heart, because reconciliation and unity are a part of God's beautiful gospel, and because Scripture casts a vision for a many-colored church family living as one. I encourage you to read this book with an open Bible and an open heart. Gray will help you see the racially divided church and world through God's eyes, and he will equip you to hear the call to become a faithful reconciler in the name of Jesus.

NIJAY K. GUPTA, professor of New Testament at Northern Seminary

How to Heal Our Racial Divide by Pastor Derwin Gray has given me a new category—"color-blessed." In the body of Christ, it is a sacred *blessing* for us as diverse people to stand together as one in him. Thank you, Pastor Gray, for helping us embrace this blessing so that everyone can see Jesus really is the Prince of Peace.

RAY ORTLUND, president of Renewal Ministries, Nashville

In a world where we can't even agree on how to talk about racism or why it matters, pastor and theologian Derwin Gray takes us back to the heart of God. From Abraham to Jesus, from Babel to Pentecost, Gray unpacks the biblical vision of God's plan to create a single, worldwide, multiethnic family in Jesus Christ. Full of theological depth, personal vulnerability, and pastoral guidance, this book is a Spirit-breathed manifesto for our cultural moment, a clarion call for the church to be, by the grace of God, all that we were called and redeemed to be.

REV. DR. GLENN PACKIAM, associate senior pastor of New Life Church, Colorado Springs, and author of *The Resilient Pastor* and *Blessed Broken Given*

Derwin Gray has been a trusted teacher and guide for me on my journey toward understanding racial unity and reconciliation. His prophetic voice is needed now more than ever, and I trust these pages will bring healing and clarity to a divided world.

BRADY BOYD, senior pastor of New Life Church, Colorado Springs, and author of *Addicted to Busy* and *Extravagant*

This book is phenomenal. Every Christian needs to read this, and every pastor needs to take their church through this book. Just *wow*! If you are going to read one book on healing the racial divide, read this book, and then give a copy to everyone you know. In *How to Heal Our Racial Divide*, Derwin writes as both a theologian and practitioner, showing us that "gospel-shaped racial reconciliation and racial justice is the natural overflow of life in Christ."

CHRISTINE CAINE, founder of A21 and Propel Women

Many in our society are ignoring the church's voice when it comes to the most important and divisive issues of our day. There are two reasons. First, many of the church leaders addressing these issues are merely echoing and amplifying angry culture war rhetoric. And second, far too many church leaders are afraid to say anything at all. Thank God for Derwin Gray. Driven by neither anger nor fear, he wisely draws from Scripture to show us both the evil of racism and the healing that is possible through Jesus Christ. With thoughtfulness born from pastoral experience, Dr. Gray's is a voice both the church and our society needs to hear right now.

SKYE JETHANI, cohost of *The Holy Post* podcast and author of WithGodDaily.com

This is the book I've been waiting for on racial reconciliation. Not written by an activist, historian, or sociologist but a pastor who sees it all through the lens of the gospel. He writes as he lives and preaches—to the whole body of Christ. Nothing is left out. Would to God that I'd had this book when we started intentionally integrating Northwood Church.

BOB ROBERTS, global senior pastor of Northwood Church, founder of Glocal.net, and cofounder of Multi-Faith Neighbors Network

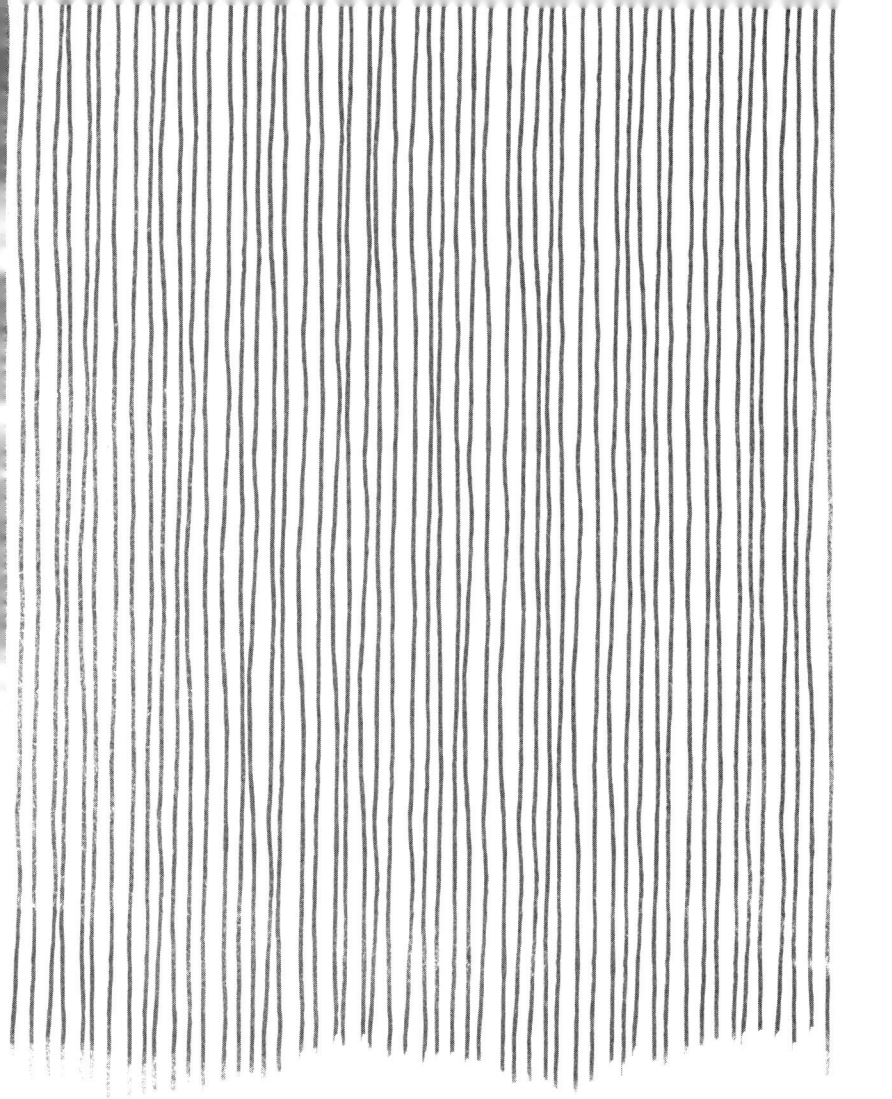

HOW TO HEAL OUR RACIAL DIVIDE

HOW TO HEAL OUR RACIAL DIVIDE

WHAT THE BIBLE SAYS, AND THE FIRST CHRISTIANS KNEW, ABOUT RACIAL RECONCILIATION

DERWIN L. GRAY

TYNDALE
MOMENTUM®

A Tyndale nonfiction imprint

Visit Tyndale online at tyndale.com.

Visit Tyndale Momentum online at tyndalemomentum.com.

Tyndale, Tyndale's quill logo, *Tyndale Momentum*, and the Tyndale Momentum logo are registered trademarks of Tyndale House Ministries. Tyndale Momentum is a nonfiction imprint of Tyndale House Publishers, Carol Stream, Illinois.

How to Heal Our Racial Divide: What the Bible Says, and the First Christians Knew, about Racial Reconciliation

Designed by Faceout Studio, Spencer Fuller

Edited by Jonathan Schindler

Published in association with The Bindery Agency, www.TheBinderyAgency.com.

For information about special discounts for bulk purchases, please contact Tyndale House Publishers at csresponse@tyndale.com, or call 1-855-277-9400.

Library of Congress Cataloging-in-Publication Data

A catalog record for this book is available from the Library of Congress.

ISBN 978-1-4964-5880-3

Printed in the United States of America

28 27 26 25 24 23 22
7   6   5   4   3   2   1

I dedicate How to Heal Our Racial Divide *to my son, Jeremiah. Son, the sincerity of your faith in Jesus, your love for people, and your disciplined, beautiful life have always inspired me to be a better man. Thank you for the gift of your friendship. I love you. I am so proud of you.*

Contents

Foreword

It was the murder of Ahmaud Arbery for me.

I can't quite pin down why it was that particular story, the death of that young black man, that broke open my heart in a way that it hasn't ever recovered. And God willing, it never will.

Maybe it is because I grew up in Georgia and know the town well where that story happened. Maybe it is because they always show Ahmaud's senior picture when they talk about his death, and it's the same senior picture we all took. I remember my senior portraits well—I wore soccer shorts and tennis shoes, even though my hair and makeup were done. The photographer draped a black cloth over my shoulders, so it looked like I was wearing a dress. Spoiler alert: I wasn't. And so when they show that picture of him, I imagine Ahmaud, in that tuxedo top, maybe athletic shorts and running shoes just out of frame. Maybe it's that. Or maybe it was the civilian nature of the whole thing, with no law enforcement involved.

It is probably all of that combined, with my own journey and upbringing and friendships speaking into it too.

But what I know is when someone asks, "What made you start really learning and listening and wanting to be a part of the racial reconciliation story?" I say, "Ahmaud." May he rest in peace.

I bet we all have an answer to that question, because I don't think you'd pick up this book by my friend Derwin if you didn't. If you weren't already hoping things could be different, if you weren't already burdened or saddened by the social injustice that is apparent in our churches and schools and neighborhoods and restaurants and homes and hearts, you wouldn't even be trying.

So before you turn the page, whether you feel late to this conversation or just on time, whether you feel convicted or convinced or concerned, whether you picked this up yourself or it was handed to you, I just want to say, Well done, friend. No matter your skin tone or family history or faith story, you're doing a good thing learning and growing and pursuing peace with your brothers and sisters who do not look like the face you see in the mirror.

I hope Derwin is okay with me saying this, but it's all right if some of his words prick you or make you put the book down for a minute, or a day. It's okay if you struggle with some of it as you are learning and listening and turning the pages.

As I read, I had a few moments, a few sentences, where I felt that too. So I'm with you. It's what makes us human and healthy—to read and think and digest for ourselves and to be real about what it does in our hearts and minds and bodies as we read.

I think it's what makes relationship with Jesus really good, being honest and being willing to grow and change. Also, Jesus is all over this book because he deeply cares about all tribes, tongues, and nations being together as one.

So do you. I know you do. You picture it, like I do. A sea of people worshiping God, literally every shade of peach and tan and brown and black that you can think of, hair of every shade and texture and length. Who knows how we'll be dressed or how old we'll be, but we'll all be there and be so blessed to be surrounded by the world. Every tribe. Every tongue. Every nation.

I was moved by what I read in the pages you are about to experience. I saw things in Scripture I'd never seen before. I saw truths about God and humans and injustice and myself that were new to me but radically important. So might I just encourage you, as you start this book, to finish it. Read to the end. Learn, repent, grow, and share. You're doing a good thing here. And when you finish, you'll be different. And you'll be glad you didn't give up.

Annie F. Downs
New York Times bestselling
author of *That Sounds Fun*

THE NEW NORMAL

We are born into conflicts that we did not create. These disputes existed long before we arrived on Planet Earth. But we still have to live with their aftermath.

I remember going to a restaurant with my mom when I was about eight years old. As soon as we sat down, a disheveled White man started spewing hate-filled words at the Black people present. He screamed, "I remember a day when n—s were not allowed to eat at restaurants with us good White folk!" A Black man stood up to deal with the situation, but his wife stopped him, saying, "Baby, he's not worth it." My little-boy brain was confused, and my heart was afraid. Sadly, my mother grew up in a time when Black people could not eat at restaurants with White people. She remembers drinking from "colored-only" water fountains.

In elementary school, nearly every day when I walked past the last house on the block that led to my school, a thirty-something Hispanic man would shout through his screen door, "N—, Blacky, Blacky!" Before writing this book,

I hadn't thought about that experience in years. I guess my brain buried this trauma in the "let's not remember this" file. Sadly, I had normalized these types of racial slurs. That same man and his adult friends who lived with him later threatened one of my teenage Black friends by putting a knife in his face after they stole his boom box.

My friends weren't always on the receiving end of these slurs. In my preteen years, my Hispanic friends who had been born in America would use racial slurs to disparage the undocumented Mexicans who came to America illegally.

I had normalized this senseless racism. I cringe at the thought that I allowed other human beings made in the image of God to be called such dehumanizing names in my presence. But this was my normal, everyday existence.

These memories are just a drop in the sea of the daily experiences of people of every sort who live with the reality of racism, sexism, classism, and hate. Sin is ugly, and it makes us ugly to one another. Our world is a battle zone that reeks of generational, institutional discrimination and personal contempt.

Time for a New Normal

You are probably reading this book because you want to make a difference. I wrote this book because I want to make a difference too. Like you, my soul is weary from the racial divide in the church and in our country. We want to heal the hurt, right the wrongs, and create trust where distrust exists.

As a person of goodwill, you want to see change, and I want to help you become the change you want to see. Racism and racial injustice are sins so deeply embedded in our culture that it is going to require disciples of Jesus who thoroughly rely on the Holy Spirit and who passionately inhabit Jesus' love to change things.

This love we are commanded to looks like the cross of Jesus. God's kind of love moves beyond words to actions, beyond sentimental feelings to a relentless commitment to the well-being of others, and beyond comfort to uncomfortable sacrifice. In learning to love people of other ethnicities and cultural expressions, we are forged into true disciples of Jesus. By our love for one another—especially those from a different ethnicity and social class—we become a foretaste of God's Kingdom. Jesus told his disciples, "I give you a new command: Love one another. Just as I have loved you, you are also to love one another. By this everyone will know that you are my disciples, if you love one another" (John 13:34-35). The moment we say yes to Jesus as our Redeemer and King, we are enrolled in his school of love.

Jesus' disciple John writes, "The one who loves his brother or sister remains in the light, and there is no cause for stumbling in him. But the one who hates his brother or sister is in the darkness, walks in the darkness, and doesn't know where he's going, because the darkness has blinded his eyes" (1 John 2:10-11). In Christ Jesus, your brothers and sisters are Asian, Latino, White, Native, and Black people. Your being "in Christ" means your inclusion into a redeemed, multicolored, multiethnic family that God promised to Abraham.[1] Fighting against the sin of racism and racial injustice is not optional for those who call on the name of King Jesus. The apostle Paul—a Jew—proclaimed, "I am obligated both to Greeks and barbarians, both to the wise and the foolish. . . . For I am not ashamed of the gospel, because it is the power of God for salvation to everyone who believes, first to the Jew, and also to the Greek" (Romans 1:14, 16). Paul's passion to see the unity and reconciliation of Jews and Gentiles—distinct ethnicities with centuries of enmity between them—was an imperative of the gospel, even when it caused him great harm, persecution, and ultimately death.

Love that heals the racial divide is more than social-media posts or one-off events. This Holy Spirit–generated love forms us into "living sacrifices" at the altar of God's transformative grace (Romans 12:1). Only those willing to lay down their cultural power and privilege for the marginalized, oppressed, and disenfranchised will be able to love with a fierceness that unites brothers and sisters across ethnic and socioeconomic lines.

What Will You Experience?

As we walk together through the pages of this book, I am going to talk about Jesus, his gospel of grace, and his Kingdom a lot because he has a lot to say about how to heal our racial divide. You will learn that the gospel of King Jesus breaks down barriers that divide and builds up unity in God's multiethnic family, and you will discover that this is not a peripheral issue but is at the very heart of the gospel. Bible scholar N. T. Wright writes,

> Paul is referring to the new reality, accomplished in the Messiah's death and resurrection, that, because the dark powers had been overcome and new creation launched, and because of the gift of the Messiah's Spirit, all believers of whatever background stood on level ground within the community. The theology and praxis of a church united across the traditional boundaries of ethnic, class, and gender distinctions was never for Paul a secondary matter: it was at the very heart. Otherwise, one would in effect be saying that the Messiah did not after all defeat (through his death) the powers of darkness that divide and corrupt the human race.[2]

You will catch the Bible's vision for a loving, unified church that comprises all ethnicities, and you will be equipped to love your brothers and sisters of other ethnicities or socioeconomic classes. I will help you leverage your life on behalf of your brothers and sisters of another ethnicity in pursuit of racial reconciliation and racial justice.

You and your friends will discover unique and innovative ways to implement what you are learning from my book, as each chapter includes a section for you to marinate in the ideas of the chapter through prayer, thoughts, discussion questions, and practices. This holy pursuit of gospel-shaped racial reconciliation and racial justice is the natural overflow of life in Christ. This is a vital aspect of your spiritual formation, which is why I spend the second half of this book exploring what color-blessed discipleship looks like today. Jesus came to forgive and reconcile humanity to his Father so we can be reconciled to and unified with one another as siblings by the Spirit's power and presence. We are the Jesus-indwelled family that brings heaven to earth as the temple of God the Holy Spirit. We are the Spirit-enabled family that is to be salt and light, glorifying our Father in heaven.

You are going to discover that God has always wanted a multiethnic family to serve as a sign and foretaste of his Kingdom on earth. The Father's Kingdom has Black kids, White kids, Asian kids, Indigenous kids, Latino kids, and all-kind-of-mix kids in it. God's multicolored family is indwelled by Jesus, so his ministry and mission of reconciliation, justice, and love will continue through us by the Holy Spirit's transformative work.

Thank you for walking with me. Let us become the change that we want to see in the church and in the world. Through the gospel, may we heal our racial divide as bridges of grace.

CHAPTER 1

"WHY DO YOU TALK ABOUT RACE SO MUCH?"

Have you ever had a good day turn into a bad day?

One Sunday afternoon, I was marinating in my home office, reflecting on the epicness of our Sunday service at Transformation Church, where I am lead pastor and cofounder, along with my wife, Vicki.

The music was doxological.

Jesus was exalted.

I preached my guts out.

I was faithful to exegete the text.

The gospel was proclaimed.

I was feeling good when I heard the notification that I had gotten a new email. I just knew it was going to be from someone whose life had been changed by Jesus through the ministry of Transformation Church. I opened the email, and the first thing I read was "Why do you talk about race so much in your sermons? You need to stop it!"

My heart sank. That empty pit feeling entered my stomach. Doubt crept into my mind. I had to take a step back and remember who I am in Christ and whose I am in Christ.

Over the years of shepherding people, I have learned through much prayer and reliance on my wife's and other elder-pastors' wisdom to always respond to critical emails with love, patience, and theological integrity. Sometimes hostile emails are ways for professing Christians to cuss me out and say slanderous, ugly things. But other times they become pathways to understanding, reconciliation, and unity.

As Jesus' blood-purchased people "from every tribe and language and people and nation" (Revelation 5:9), we must hold people's hands and walk with them into the promised land of unity.

So I wrote the gentleman back and requested a meeting with him to discuss his email. As we sat down, I opened in prayer and assured him of my love for him and my desire to answer his question.

And as we talked, I gave him my answer. I talk about race so much because the Bible talks about it. A lot.

Many of my White siblings in Christ that join us from homogeneous churches are surprised, caught off guard, and uncomfortable with how much the Bible talks about race. Many have never seen a connection between the gospel and racism. They've been discipled to think that the gospel is only about saving souls and sending people to heaven when they die.

But I contend that racial reconciliation in Christ is not peripheral to the gospel, an optional "nice to have" or a fad issue, but central to Christ's mission and God's plan.[1] God has always promised a multicolored, multiethnic family to Abraham, and that family was given to him in Jesus Christ.

History Informs the Present

Most followers of Jesus have no idea of the ethnic tension, division, and hatred that existed in the world in which Jesus lived. Sociologist Rodney Stark describes this environment. He writes that "one of the major reasons why Greco-Roman cities were so prone to riots" was deep-seated racial conflicts and hatred.[2] Racism and racial injustice are diseases that have plagued humanity since sin entered the world and dark power proved evil. Ethnic conflicts leading to riots are not just modern phenomena.

In the biblical language, anyone who was not Jewish or a descendant of the twelve tribes of Israel was a Gentile. For Jews in the time of Jesus, the pagan, Gentile Romans ruled Israel and most of the known world with an iron fist. Many of the Jewish people in Israel and throughout the Roman world would have felt like God had abandoned them.

When they saw Gentiles, the entire history of the Jewish people would have reminded them that the Gentile

Egyptians held their ancestors as slaves for four hundred years and that Pharaoh had ordered the murder of their male babies because their population was growing too fast.[3] In this case, fear of losing power and privilege drove Pharaoh to commit murder.

Similarly, Jewish history would have reminded a Jew of Jesus' time that the Gentile Amorites, Perizzites, Canaanites, Hittites, Girgashites, Hivites, and Jebusites had waged war against them and tried to keep them from entering the land God had promised them. They would have been reminded of their ancestors' captivity in Assyria and Babylon and how the evil Gentile Haman wanted to wipe all Jews from the face of the earth.[4] If not for Queen Esther, who was a Jew, Haman would have carried out his genocidal fantasy.

History is never really history. It has a way of informing our present.

For the Jews of the first century, living under Roman rule, history voiced to them that the Gentiles were not to be trusted. For many Jews, Gentiles were their enemies and a threat to their religious life. The apostle Peter reflected a common Jewish attitude of the time when he told the Gentile Cornelius, "You know it is against our laws for a Jewish man to enter a Gentile home like this or to associate with you" (Acts 10:28, NLT). In some aspects of Jewish life, it was normative that a Jewish man could not enter a Gentile home. Segregation also is not new to our modern world.

It was in this racially charged and divided world that Jesus created an alternative community of unity called the

Kingdom of God and that the gospel forged a path that led to healing. God can bring different groups of people together and bring healing to our racial divide today if we are willing to obey Jesus and live out his gospel. Ultimate unity will come in the new heaven and new earth; God's people point to that future by our unity in the present.

A Vision of Transformation

On August 2, 1997, I met Jesus in a small dorm room at Anderson University during my fifth training camp with the Indianapolis Colts. A teammate named Steve Grant had spent five years sowing seeds of the gospel in my heart. Every day after practice, he would take a shower, dry off, wrap a white towel around his waist, and ask my teammates, "Do you know Jesus?" His nickname was the Naked Preacher. God used him to bring me to faith.

I called my wife, Vicki, and said, "I want to be more committed to you, and I want to be committed to Jesus." For the first time, I knew that I was loved and forgiven. I knew that I was new.

Vicki had met Jesus a few months before I did through the love of one of her coworkers, Karen Ponish. Both of us fell in love with Jesus. We loved reading the Bible. We just wanted to know him more and make him known. If he could transform our lives, he had the power to transform anyone's life.

As we spent time diving into Scripture, we quickly became aware of how much the Bible talks about Jesus forgiving people, loving people, and bringing people of different ethnicities together as a family. We were in awe as we read the words of the apostle Paul:

> In those days you were living apart from Christ. You were excluded from citizenship among the people of Israel, and you did not know the covenant promises God had made to them. You lived in this world without God and without hope. But now you have been united with Christ Jesus. Once you were far away from God, but now you have been brought near to him through the blood of Christ.
>
> For Christ himself has brought peace to us. He united Jews and Gentiles into one people when, in his own body on the cross, he broke down the wall of hostility that separated us. He did this by ending the system of law with its commandments and regulations. He made peace between Jews and Gentiles by creating in himself one new people from the two groups. Together as one body, Christ reconciled both groups to God by means of his death on the cross, and our hostility toward each other was put to death.
>
> EPHESIANS 2:12-16, NLT

When Vicki (a White woman) and I (a Black man) read these verses, it was just so clear. Jesus cares about healing our racial divide. The God who makes us new is the God who makes a new family that is colorful and diverse. But then reality quickly set in and dampened our excitement. We started looking for churches like the ones the New Testament describes. Unfortunately, we found that churches were divided over race! It was like we were forced to choose a Black church or a White church. Why was the nightclub more ethnically diverse than Jesus' club, the church?

That's why my wife and I began praying, dreaming, and preparing to plant a church where White, Asian, Black, Indigenous, and Latino people of diverse ages and economic backgrounds could find a community to belong to. We dreamed of a church united in Jesus through his gospel, embodying his Kingdom.

I envisioned CEOs being in small groups with elementary school teachers. I saw people who lived in trailer parks discipling people who lived in the suburbs. I saw White police officers and police officers of color leading a small group of ethnically diverse teens in understanding the gospel. I saw Black people who were suspicious of White people and White people who were suspicious of Black people becoming trusted friends and family. I saw a mosaic of people loving God and each other so beautifully that the world had to take note. I could see Transformation Church equipping people to be the healing they wanted to see in the world. I imagined a church that, if it did not exist, the community would miss because Jesus was present in us.

Jesus is the King of his Kingdom. And in his Kingdom are people of all ethnicities that bear God's image. It is a holy, unified, blood-bought family. Jesus' vision captured our hearts and wouldn't let go.

The Bible Is Not Colorless

So when people ask me why I talk about race in my sermons, I describe it this way:

The reason I preach about race so much is that the Bible does.

The reason I preach against the sin of racism so much is that the Bible does.

The reason I preach ethnic unity in the church so much is that the Bible does.

The reason I preach about ethnic unity so much is that Jesus and the apostle Paul did. Paul even went so far as to say that when God's people are unified across ethnic lines, the demonic realm is put on notice that Jesus has won the battle.[5]

According to Paul, ethnic unity among his children is an eternal desire of God's heart. God has forever purposed through Jesus' sinless life, sacrificial death on the cross, and resurrection to create a multiethnic family. Racism, racial injustice, and disunity are invasive parasites that must be eradicated from his church.

The Bible is not colorless; rather, it is full of different ethnicities across the Old and New Testaments. If we take ethnicity out of the Bible, Jesus would not be a Jew, the woman at the well would not be a Samaritan, Pharaoh would not be an Egyptian, Cornelius would not be an Italian, Pilate would not be a Roman, and there would be no Amorites, Perizzites, Canaanites, Hittites, Girgashites, Hivites, and Jebusites. It wouldn't matter that Jonah was called to preach to the Assyrians. There would be no story about the Good Samaritan. There would no Ethiopian eunuch. There would be no Revelation 5:9-10:

And they sang a new song:

You are worthy to take the scroll
and to open its seals,
because you were slaughtered,
and you purchased people
for God by your blood
from every tribe and language
and people and nation.
You made them a kingdom
and priests to our God,
and they will reign on the earth.

Our ethnicity is a gift from God reflecting his multifaceted wisdom. Biblical characters are not colorless or cultureless. They were people situated in real places, in real image-bearing ethnicities, in particular cultures and times—just as we are. God's Word cannot be faithfully interpreted and understood without understanding the sociohistorical reality of ethnicity and culture and the corruptive, destructive nature of sin. Sin, as it lives in the hearts of humanity and in the systems and societies we put in place, has pitted humanity against God and humanity against one another. If we strip the Bible of ethnicity and cultural context and implications, we are left with an individualistic gospel that is only concerned with saving our own souls.

In 1963, Dr. Martin Luther King Jr. addressed just this problem in his magisterial "Letter from a Birmingham Jail":

> In the midst of blatant injustices inflicted upon the Negro, I have watched white churchmen stand on the sideline and mouth pious irrelevancies and sanctimonious trivialities. In the midst of a mighty struggle to rid our nation of racial and economic injustice, I have heard many ministers say: "Those are social issues, with which the gospel has no real concern." And I have watched many churches commit themselves to a completely other worldly religion which makes a strange, un-Biblical distinction between body and soul, between the sacred and the secular.[6]

At Transformation Church, we believe—with the Bible as our guide—that ethnic reconciliation is intrinsic to discipleship. Jesus desires for his people—from all ethnicities and cultures—to love each other well. Jesus says, "May they all be one, as you, Father, are in me and I am in you. May they also be in us, so that the world may believe you sent me" (John 17:21). Our oneness bears witness to the reality that

Jesus was sent by the Father. We become a living testimony. The longer we allow our racial divides to persist, the harder it becomes to resist the powers that seek to destroy us and distract us from God's glory.

That's why I've written this book. Scripture paints a picture of unity that has already been accomplished in Jesus' work on the cross. The way to heal our racial divide is to catch the Bible's vision of a new community—a multiethnic community—formed around King Jesus in mutual love. In the first part of this book, we'll walk through the Bible and see how this was God's plan all along. And in the second part, we'll look at how this vision might be lived out today in color-blessed (rather than colorblind) discipleship.

God Promised Abraham a Family

Jesus wants to save more than our souls. As we journey together, we will showcase just how majestic, beautiful, and all-encompassing Jesus' salvation truly is. We are going to marvel at his brilliance and creative genius that not only forgives our sins but also creates a beautifully diverse family with different-colored skins. We will become color-blessed, not colorblind. This new blood-bought, regenerated, multicolored family is the one God promised Abraham long ago:

> Now the Scripture saw in advance that God would
> justify the Gentiles by faith and proclaimed the
> gospel ahead of time to Abraham, saying, All the

nations will be blessed through you. Consequently, those who have faith are blessed with Abraham, who had faith.

GALATIANS 3:8-9

Jesus, the Jewish Messiah, is the Savior of *all* humanity. With love in his eyes and grace in his nail-pierced hands, he came to earth to give his Father the family he promised Abraham. This family is called the church, the body of Christ. Jesus' passion to see his Father's children live in unity and beauty is rooted in God's covenant with Abraham. This is a redemptive aspect of the gospel that is often neglected: "He redeemed us in order that the blessing given to Abraham might come to the Gentiles through Christ Jesus, so that by faith we might receive the promise of the Spirit" (Galatians 3:14, NIV).

One of the miracles of the early church was its barrier-breaking, reconciling nature. Jesus birthed a new society, composed of unlikely participants—Jews and Gentiles, rich and poor, male and female:

In Christ there is not Greek and Jew, circumcision and uncircumcision, barbarian, Scythian, slave and free; but Christ is all and in all.

COLOSSIANS 3:11

There is no Jew or Greek, slave or free, male and female; since you are all one in Christ Jesus. And if you belong to Christ, then you are Abraham's seed, heirs according to the promise.

GALATIANS 3:28-29

For we were all baptized by one Spirit into one body—whether Jews or Greeks, whether slaves or free—and we were all given one Spirit to drink.

I CORINTHIANS 12:13

The apostle Paul was constantly harassed, persecuted, and slandered because he preached the reality that Gentiles were full members of God's family. Jews, as well as Gentiles, considered Paul's desire to heal the ethnic divide worthy of death. At one point, he was speaking to a crowd of Jews, telling of his Jewish heritage and his persecution of Christians until God intervened on the road to Damascus:

"[The Lord] said to me, 'Go, because I will send you far away to the Gentiles.'"
They listened to him up to this point. Then they raised their voices, shouting, "Wipe this man off the face of the earth! He should not be allowed to live!"

ACTS 22:21-22

For Paul, the message of unity between Jews and Gentiles in Abraham's family was seen as a threat. Today, not much has changed as it relates to reconciling people of different ethnicities.

HOW TO HEAL OUR RACIAL DIVIDE

If you choose to become a uniter, many of your friends will become enemies.

You will be slandered.

You will be persecuted.

You will be called an agitating race-baiter.

You will be called "woke" or worse, a communist.

You will be called a sellout to your own race.

But, most importantly, you will also be called faithful to Jesus, his gospel, and his Kingdom.

The hard, gospel work of healing the racial divide in the church and in our nation is going to cost you something personally. But whatever the cost, Jesus and his glory are worth it. Our pursuit of Jesus and his purpose to see his people unified will lead to "weaknesses, insults, hardships, persecutions, and . . . difficulties, for the sake of Christ." But this is not a bad thing, for, as the apostle Paul tells us, "when I am weak, then I am strong" (2 Corinthians 12:10). Paul also writes, "I bear on my body the marks of Jesus" (Galatians 6:17). At the end of your life and mine, may we, too, bear the marks of Jesus because we lived sacrificially, laying down our lives to unite people in Christ.

| | | | | **MARINATE ON THIS** | | | | |

PRAYER

Father,

I look at all the anger, division, and hatred that seems to be everywhere.

I want to do something, but I am not sure what to do.

Racism and racial injustice are crimes against you and humanity.

Ethnic disunity in your church hurts your heart.

Lord Jesus,

Show me how to love like you do.

Teach me how to heal the racial divide in my own heart and in the world.

You loved all people. I want to love like you.

Holy Spirit,

I need a power beyond myself. Just as you blew the wind of life into the early church,

blow the winds of grace into the sails of my life

so I can be a uniter, not a divider; a healer, not a hurter.

I pray this in Jesus' name,

Amen.

THINGS TO THINK ABOUT

- As Jesus' blood-purchased people "from every tribe and language and people and nation" (Revelation 5:9), we must hold people's hands and walk with them into the promised land of unity.

- The reason I preach about race so much is that the Bible does. The reason I preach against racism so much is that the Bible does.

- Our ethnicity is a gift from God reflecting his multi-faceted wisdom (see Ephesians 3:10).

QUESTIONS TO DISCUSS

1. Read Revelation 5:9. What has been your experience with race and ethnicity in the church? How does it compare to the picture we see in Revelation?

2. Biblical characters are not colorless or cultureless. They were people situated in real places, in real image-bearing ethnicities, in particular cultures and times—just like we are. When you read the Bible, what examples of ethnicity and culture do you see? Why are these important?

3. In what ways does your ethnicity and culture shape your faith or how you read the Bible?

4. Read Ephesians 3:4-11. How is our ethnicity a gift?

GOSPEL BEHAVIORS TO PRACTICE

Find another Christian (of another ethnicity, if possible) to read through this book with you. Discuss what you hope to get out of reading this book and how you might spur one another on to unite people in Christ.

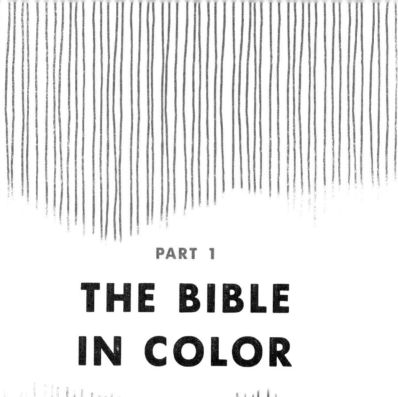

PART 1

THE BIBLE
IN COLOR

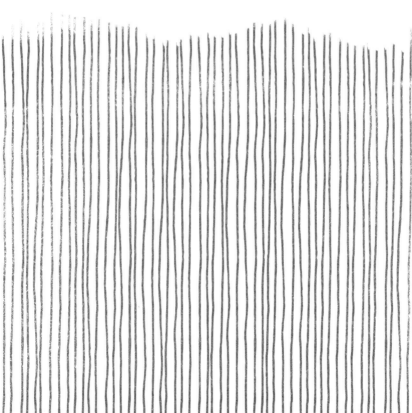

CHAPTER 2

A FAMILY FOR ABRAHAM

In this portion of the book, we will look at what the Bible has to say, and the first Christians knew, about racial reconciliation. We will look at specific stories and events from the life of Jesus and the New Testament church that will help us to understand God's heart for ethnic unity, as well as the way these reflect the Old Testament's vision. But before we do that, we need to get a broader perspective of the grand sweep of the Bible's story.

Somewhere along the way, somehow, there is a name that has been forgotten in the American church. If we remember this man's name and God's promise to him, we can experience the deep ethnic reconciliation that the cross of Jesus secured. The man's name is Abraham, and he is the father of many nations (which, as we will see, means many ethnicities):

> When Abram was ninety-nine years old, the LORD appeared to him, saying, "I am God Almighty. Live in my presence and be blameless. I will set up my covenant between me and you, and I will multiply you greatly."
>
> Then Abram fell facedown and God spoke with him: "As for me, here is my covenant with you: You will become the father of many nations. Your name will no longer be Abram; your name will be Abraham, for I will make you the father of many nations."
>
> GENESIS 17:1-5

In Abraham's promised family, Jews and the rest of God's worldwide family of different ethnicities "are coheirs, members of the same body, and partners in the promise in Christ Jesus through the gospel" (Ephesians 3:6). Jesus kept his Father's promise to Abraham through his life, death, and resurrection and through his victory over sin, death, and the powers of darkness. You are a product of the promise-keeping God, and so are your ethnically diverse siblings. Love and unity across ethnic lines were secured at the cross of Christ.

We may be tempted to think about ethnic unity purely in terms of the early church, but contemplate the words of Christopher J. H. Wright:

The link [between the people of God and the
mission of God] must be traced much further
back than Pentecost but right back into the Old
Testament. The New Testament church may have
been birthed that day, but the people of God in
history go back to Abraham. And as Paul was
fond of pointing out to all and sundry, any person
of any nation who is in Christ is thereby also in
Abraham.[1]

God has always longed to have a single, worldwide, multinational, multiethnic family of coheirs and equals in Christ,
who love him by loving each other. At the heart of ethnic
reconciliation is *God's* heart for the reconciliation of people
and creation. God's gospel has created and secured our reconciliation with him and each other across ethnic barriers. Jesus,
"the visible image of the invisible God," calls us to reconciliation.[2] Ponder the words of Paul:

God in all his fullness
    was pleased to live in Christ,
and through him God reconciled
    everything to himself.
He made peace with everything in
        heaven and on earth
    by means of Christ's blood on
        the cross.

COLOSSIANS 1:19-20, NLT

The bloody cross of Jesus has reconciling power. The word "reconciled" here (from the Greek *apokatallassō*) means to restore and create harmony in a relationship. The blood of Jesus will reconcile the universe. And God's people are to be reconciled to him and each other in harmony. This is not a side issue. This is intrinsic to the gospel. This gospel reality helped the ethnically divided Jew-Gentile congregations in the New Testament era grow in healing their racial divide, and it can help us today as well.

A Word on the Terms *Race* and *Ethnicity*

Before we begin, we need to take a quick look at the terms *race* and *ethnicity*. These words are often used interchangeably; however, they have different meanings. *Ethnicity* is a word deeply rooted in the Bible. Lisa Sharon Harper writes,

> *Ethnicity* is biblical (Hebrew: *goy* or *am*; Greek: *ethnos*). Ethnicity is created by God as people groups move together through space and time. Ethnicity is dynamic and developed over long periods of time. It is not about power. It is about group identity, heritage, language, place, and common group experience. . . . Ethnicity is God's very good intention for humanity.[3]

The term *race*, by contrast, as a category has no scientific justification and no basis in biological sciences. It is a sociologically created category used more commonly to establish a caste system of power and domination over those who are viewed as inferior. In America, race is mostly defined by skin color and other physical features.[4]

Ultimately, there is only one race—the human race—that is composed of a beautiful array of ethnicities, all in need of redemption. Paul says as much in his sermon in Athens:

> *From one man* he [God] has made *every nationality* [*ethnos*] to live over the whole earth and has determined their appointed times and the boundaries of where they live. He did this so that they might seek God, and perhaps they might reach out and find him, though he is not far from each one of us.
>
> ACTS 17:26-27, EMPHASIS ADDED

Throughout this book, I will use both *race* and *ethnicity* in their familiar contexts, such as "racial reconciliation" or "ethnic diversity," but keep in mind that the Bible's concern is with uniting all of God's many children of all ethnicities into one family—Abraham's family. In the biblical language, all non-Jews are Gentiles, so unless you are ethnically Jewish, that means you. Thankfully, Jesus came to redeem, regenerate, and reconcile all people to his Abba and to each other so we can love as he does. This is God's glorious intent for us.

> And this is God's plan: Both Gentiles and Jews who believe the Good News share equally in the riches inherited by God's children. Both are part of the

same body, and both enjoy the promise of blessings
because they belong to Christ Jesus.

EPHESIANS 3:6, NLT

God Called Abraham So LIFE Could Flourish

The living and loving Creator of all is Life himself. The God
of the Scriptures invites his children to share in his limitless,
eternal life. This life is a life of union with God, expressing his
image and fulfilling his will on earth as it is in heaven. As we
consider Abraham's connection to the gospel story, the acronym
LIFE will help us to remember his importance. LIFE stands for:

- Life
- Inheritance
- Family
- Expression

LIFE

God called Abraham in Genesis 12:1-3 in response to what
happened in chapters 3 through 11 of Genesis. God's creation project ran off the tracks due to Adam and Eve's rebellion. And wherever there is hostility toward the Creator, the
creation will be hostile toward each other. They will raise
up arms to enslave, oppress, sexualize, and kill their fellow
image-bearers. Death invaded life, so God called Abraham,
and through his seed, death would be defeated on the cross,
and through the Resurrection, new life would be inaugurated.

The call of Abraham launched God's spectacular plan of redemption to get his creation project back on track. God's redemptive purpose culminated and was fulfilled in Jesus of Nazareth, Israel's Messiah and the world's true King. The call of Abraham flung open the gates so that Abraham and his descendants could "bless and deliver the entire world."[5] This is the narrative the first Christians knew and lived. As a result, Jesus' church produced a unity that became the envy of Rome.

In calling Abraham, God announced the gospel to him, saying, "All the peoples on earth will be blessed through you" (Genesis 12:3). Thousands of years before the incarnation of Jesus, God promised Abraham a family comprising all peoples or nations.[6] God's covenant with Abraham is of epic importance to him; therefore, it must be of great importance to those of us who call upon the name of Jesus. The saving work of Jesus gave Abraham a sin-forgiven family from different cultures and ethnicities.

As the Galatian church struggled with the sin of ethnic supremacy and disunity between the Jews and Gentiles, the apostle Paul wrote the following:

You know, then, that those who have faith, these are Abraham's sons. Now the Scripture saw in advance that God would justify the Gentiles by faith and proclaimed the gospel ahead of time to Abraham, saying, All the nations will be blessed through you.

Consequently, those who have faith are blessed with
Abraham, who had faith.

GALATIANS 3:7-9

Before you move on, read Galatians 3:7-9 again.

Did you catch it?

In this key passage, Paul combines four gospel truths that
will help us heal the racial divide:

- "the promise of God
- the faith of Abraham
- the universal mission of God to bless all nations
  through the seed of Abraham
- the saving implications for all who have faith like
  Abraham"[7]

Christopher J. H. Wright comments on this passage,
"*This*, says Paul—this dynamic narrative of God's saving
purpose for all nations through Abraham—is the heart of
the gospel as announced by the Scriptures."[8] The narrative of
God is one of a loving Father who sends his Son on a mission of reconciliation through the Spirit's power to rescue his
children from slavery to sin and death. Sin and death divide,
but Jesus' victory over sin, death, and the dark powers of evil
unites us vertically to God and horizontally to each other. The
redeemed, interethnic family for Abraham was birthed out
of the blood of the crucified and risen Messiah and through
the promised Holy Spirit: "Through Christ Jesus, God has

blessed the Gentiles with the same blessing he promised to Abraham, so that we who are believers might receive the promised Holy Spirit through faith" (Galatians 3:14, NLT).

True life—the life that flows from Abraham's seed, the Messiah Jesus[9]—is the very life of God himself. The Bible calls possessing this life being "born again."[10] Those who call on Jesus are reborn and united to Jesus and each other. Please do not miss the "united to each other" part. We are redeemed individually and placed into the corporate, communal body of Christ. We are born again into a new community, a new society of people that pulsates with the resurrection life of Jesus and the sealing work of God the Spirit.

Paul and the early church affirmed this promise: "Now that you belong to Christ, you are the true children of Abraham. You are his heirs, and God's promise to Abraham belongs to you" (Galatians 3:29, NLT). It's time that we affirm it also.

Life in Christ raises us from spiritual death so we can participate and share in the tripersonal life of God. Not only does his eternal life secure our *redemptive unity*, but it also gives us an *inheritance*.

INHERITANCE

As Abraham's colorful kids in Christ, we eagerly look forward to our inheritance. Our inheritance is not just the land of Canaan, promised to Abraham's physical descendants. God's new worldwide family inherits the whole world.[11] God's "every nation and tribe and tongue" people are recreated for the new world that Jesus launched at his resurrection.[12] Therefore, *we are to represent the future in the present.* Just as God's people are under construction, formed as clay is shaped by the potter, so is the world we will inherit. This process is called progressive sanctification. It is the power of God's Spirit working in the new people of God to conform us to Jesus, the Son of God.[13] As we obey the Spirit's work in us and are matured into Christlikeness, we are empowered by the indwelling life of Jesus to "lead a life worthy of [our] calling," treating each other with humility, gentleness, patience, forgiveness, and love. Compelled by the gospel, we "make every effort" in the Spirit's power to keep ourselves united, "binding [ourselves] together with peace" (Ephesians 4:1-3, NLT).

Paul uses his gospel-drenched pen to paint a picture of our inheritance:

> All creation is waiting eagerly for that future day
> when God will reveal who his children really are.
> Against its will, all creation was subjected to God's
> curse. But with eager hope, the creation looks
> forward to the day when it will join God's children
> in glorious freedom from death and decay. For we
> know that all creation has been groaning as in the
> pains of childbirth right up to the present time.
> And we believers also groan, even though we have
> the Holy Spirit within us as a foretaste of future
> glory, for we long for our bodies to be released from

sin and suffering. We, too, wait with eager hope for
the day when God will give us our full rights as his
adopted children, including the new bodies he has
promised us.

ROMANS 8:19-23, NLT

The vision of our glorious inheritance is beautiful beyond
what our minds can conceive. Cuban American scholar
Justo L. González helps us grasp the magnificence of our
inheritance:

> There is beauty, and joy, and fullness, in many people
> coming together, out of every tribe and nation and
> people and language. . . . The vision which John the
> Jew has is a vision of a Gentile church, a church where
> the Gentiles, the nations, *ta ethne*, the *goyim*, will
> come and take their place right next to the tribes of
> Israel, and all together will claim the ancient promise
> made to the people of Israel, that they would be a
> kingdom of priests. That is a vision sweet as honey,
> for it shows the fullness of the mercy of God.[14]

This is gospel truth, secured through the life, death, and
resurrection of Messiah Jesus, in fulfillment of God's covenant with Abraham. There is no ethnic supremacy, political idolatry, Christian nationalism, and racism in the future
that all believers in Christ will inherit and share. Therefore,
let us practice our future together now, in the present. In view

of God's mercy, will you become a living sacrifice and obey Jesus, allowing his vision of the future to transform how you live and love today? Paul describes this vision:

> This is the plan: At the right time [God] will bring everything together under the authority of Christ— everything in heaven and on earth. Furthermore, because we are united with Christ, we have received an inheritance from God, for he chose us in advance, and he makes everything work out according to his plan.
>
> God's purpose was that we Jews who were the first to trust in Christ would bring praise and glory to God. And now you Gentiles have also heard the truth, the Good News that God saves you. And when you believed in Christ, he identified you as his own by giving you the Holy Spirit, whom he promised long ago. The Spirit is God's guarantee that he will give us the inheritance he promised and that he has purchased us to be his own people. He did this so we would praise and glorify him.
>
> EPHESIANS 1:10-14, NLT

The people of Abraham share the resurrection life of Jesus and inherit a glorious future. This promise is not just for individuals, but for the corporate body of the Messiah: the multiethnic, reconciled family of Abraham.

FAMILY

Before there were days, in the deep recesses of eternity, in the Eternal One's heart,[15] it was always God's intention to give Abraham a family. This wasn't a new concept introduced by the early church. Rather, even in the Old Testament, we find evidence of God's heart to reach the nations. After God freed his people from slavery in Egypt through the Passover, "a mixed crowd also went up with them" (Exodus 12:38). The Hebrew phrase translated "a mixed crowd" (*erev rav*) "refers to a mixed group of non-Israelites who joined them in their departure."[16] In Israel's wilderness wanderings, we see Moses marrying "a Cushite woman" (Numbers 12:1). In the Old Testament, "Cush" referred to an area south of Egypt, above the Nile, "where a Black African civilization flourished for over two thousand years."[17] Moses married a Black woman.

The prophet Isaiah declared that Israel's Messiah would free the Gentiles from the "dark dungeons" of idolatry. Israel's Messiah, the world's true Lord, would "be a light to guide the nations," bringing the Gentiles into Abraham's family.[18]

During Jew-Gentile ethnic disharmony and division caused by sin and the powers of darkness, the apostle Paul reminded the church in Rome that God would create a Jew-Gentile family where Christ was supreme. Jews and Gentiles were now on equal footing in God's new, multiethnic people. And he reminded them of this fact by quoting the Old Testament four times in quick succession:

He also came so that the Gentiles might give glory
to God for his mercies to them. That is what the
psalmist meant when he wrote:

> "For this, I will praise you among the Gentiles;
>   I will sing praises to your name." [Psalm 18:49]

And in another place it is written,

> "Rejoice with his people,
>   you Gentiles." [Deuteronomy 32:43]

And yet again,

> "Praise the LORD, all you Gentiles.
>   Praise him, all you people of the earth."
>   [Psalm 117:1]

And in another place Isaiah said,

> "The heir to David's throne will come,
>   and he will rule over the Gentiles.
> They will place their hope on him." [Isaiah 11:10]

ROMANS 15:9-12, NLT

And beyond all this, within the very lineage of Israel's
Messiah, Jesus of Nazareth, are four Gentile women: Tamar,
Rahab, Ruth, and Bathsheba.[19]

These examples are not meant to be exhaustive, and there are numerous other examples of God's heart for the nations in the Old Testament (several of which will be discussed in the following three chapters). Suffice it to say, it is the testimony of Scripture, from Genesis to Revelation, that the living and loving God has always wanted to give Abraham a family from every nation and tribe and tongue. This spectacularly loved mosaic of people are siblings, coequals, and coheirs in God's Kingdom.

In our sin-divided world, the united family of Abraham is to be a living, prophetic foretaste of Jesus' victory over the dark powers of sin and death. Paul describes the triumph of Jesus with these words: "God's purpose in all this was to use the church to display his wisdom in its rich variety to all the unseen rulers and authorities in the heavenly places. This was his eternal plan, which he carried out through Christ Jesus our Lord" (Ephesians 3:10-11, NLT).

Like the early church, we must familiarize ourselves with and internalize God's story of redemption. The American church has co-opted God's story and shrunk it to an individualized, reduced salvation of Jesus dying only for *my* sins. But Jesus died for *your* sins, *my* sins, and the *world's* sins so that a forgiven, reconciled, regenerated, righteous, holy, loved, unified, and Spirit-indwelled family could be given to Abraham.[20]

Somehow we have been deceived into thinking that loving our brothers and sisters of a different ethnicity, political party, socioeconomic class, or gender is optional. Loving and living in unity is not optional. Reconciliation is intrinsic to the gospel of our King:

For Christ himself has brought peace to us. He
united Jews and Gentiles into one people when, in
his own body on the cross, he broke down the wall
of hostility that separated us. . . . He made peace
between Jews and Gentiles by creating in himself
one new people from the two groups. Together as
one body, Christ reconciled both groups to God by
means of his death on the cross, and our hostility
toward each other was put to death.

EPHESIANS 2:14-16, NLT

EXPRESSION

Through Abraham and his seed—Jesus—God gives *LIFE* to
those who trust him. The power of darkness and sin separated and divided God's children from him and from each
other. God's call to Abraham was his answer to the disease
that plagued humanity and the world. Out of Abraham,

you are all children of God through faith in Christ
Jesus. And all who have been united with Christ in
baptism have put on Christ, like putting on new
clothes. There is no longer Jew or Gentile, slave or
free, male and female. For you are all one in Christ
Jesus. And now that you belong to Christ, you are
the true children of Abraham. You are his heirs,
and God's promise to Abraham belongs to you.

GALATIANS 3:26-29, NLT

As Abraham's family, we are to express our allegiance to Jesus by relying on God the Holy Spirit to encourage, empower, and equip us to live in oneness and unity as a testimony of the gospel.

Our ethnic differences are not obliterated; in Christ, they are celebrated.

Our socioeconomic differences, in Christ, become a pathway to mutual learning and cooperation.

Our male/female differences are not blurred or erased; in Christ, they are embraced and complement one another to bring glory to God.

When Abraham's family is unified in the person of Jesus, we become a portrait of the new world that Jesus unveiled at his resurrection. God's new world is a multiethnic, reconciled world of love, unity, and oneness.

Abraham's children are a people of LIFE—life, inheritance, family, and expression.

A vision of the future transforms how we live today. May today be the day we join Jesus in healing the racial divide through the gospel that was "proclaimed . . . ahead of time to Abraham" (Galatians 3:8).

| | | | | **MARINATE ON THIS** | | | | |

PRAYER

Father,

You made a promise to Abraham.

Your promise was fulfilled by your Son and sealed by the Spirit.

*By grace through faith, I belong to this beautiful kaleidoscope
called the church.*

*In your family purchased by Jesus and birthed in the blood of
Jesus are people of different ethnicities and cultures.*

*As a member of Abraham's family, I stand in unity
and oneness with my siblings.*

*Teach me to love my family members the way Jesus
loves me.*

Teach me to pursue the unity that the blood provided.

*May we be forever united in love and harmony to the
glory of God.*

In Jesus' name,

Amen.

THINGS TO THINK ABOUT

- God called Abraham in Genesis 12:1-3, in response to Genesis 3–11. Wherever there is hostility against the Creator, the creation will be hostile toward each other. They will raise up arms to enslave, oppress, sexualize, and kill their fellow image-bearers. Death invaded life, so God defeated death by calling Abraham and his seed to inaugurate new life.

- Galatians 3:7-9 is a key passage because it describes "the promise of God, the faith of Abraham, the universal mission of God to bless all nations through the seed of Abraham, [and] the saving implications for all who have faith like Abraham." Paul is saying that "this dynamic narrative of God's saving purpose for all nations through Abraham—is the heart of the gospel as announced by the Scriptures."[21]

- God's "every nation and tribe and tongue" people are recreated for the new world that Jesus launched at his resurrection.[22] Therefore, we are to represent the future in the present.

- It is the testimony of Scripture, from Genesis to Revelation, that the living and loving God has always wanted to give Abraham a family from every nation and tribe and tongue. This spectacularly loved mosaic of people are siblings, coequals, and coheirs in God's Kingdom.

QUESTIONS TO DISCUSS

1. In Galatians 3:7-9, Paul combines four gospel truths that will help us heal the racial divide (see page 34). What are these four gospel truths? How do these truths shape our understanding of the gospel?

2. What does the acronym LIFE mean? How does LIFE mark our lives as Abraham's children?

3. Why does the conversation about healing our racial divide start with Abraham?

GOSPEL BEHAVIORS TO PRACTICE

Explain to someone you know why Abraham is essential to the gospel and healing our racial divide. Consider studying Abraham's story in Genesis 12–25 with them in more depth.

CHAPTER 3

JESUS
THE BARRIER BREAKER
AND FAMILY MAKER

Jesus is the key to rightly interpreting Scripture. When the Jewish religious leaders confronted Jesus during his ministry, he told them, "You search the Scriptures because you think they give you eternal life. But the Scriptures point to me!" (John 5:39, NLT). After his resurrection, Jesus walked with the travelers on the road to Emmaus and "took them through the writings of Moses and all the prophets, explaining from all the Scriptures the things concerning himself" (Luke 24:27, NLT). And later he told his disciples, "These are my words that I spoke to you while I was still with you—that everything written about me in the Law of Moses, the Prophets, and the Psalms must be fulfilled." And then "he opened their minds to understand the Scriptures" (Luke 24:44-45).

We can't understand Scripture rightly without knowing Jesus. He is the key. So what do Jesus' life, death, and resurrection, along with his teaching, have to tell us about healing our racial divide?

A great deal.

Jesus is the barrier breaker and the family maker, the fulfillment of God's promise to Abraham that he would be "the father of many nations" (Genesis 17:5).

A Light of Revelation

Soon after Jesus' birth, his parents took him to the Temple in Jerusalem to be dedicated and to offer a sacrifice, as was the custom. There they encountered Simeon, a devout Jewish man:

It had been revealed to [Simeon] by the Holy Spirit that he would not see death before he saw the Lord's Messiah. Guided by the Spirit, he entered the temple. When the parents brought in the child Jesus to perform for him what was customary under the law, Simeon took him up in his arms, praised God, and said,

Now, Master,
you can dismiss your servant in peace,
as you promised.

For my eyes have seen your salvation.
You have prepared it
in the presence of all peoples—
a light for revelation to the Gentiles
and glory to your people Israel.

LUKE 2:26-32

Simeon quoted a litany of Old Testament Scriptures affirming that the salvation brought forth by the Jewish Messiah was a salvation that included Gentiles.[1] However, to many Jews in Simeon's day, the Gentiles were the enemy— the unclean, the impure, the oppressor, the sexually immoral, the sinner, the pagan. Yet the Jewish Messiah had come to include them in the family God promised Abraham.

Even within Jesus' genealogy as recorded by Matthew, we get a glimpse of how God has always wanted to include Gentiles in the family he promised Abraham. In the Messiah's line, we find four Gentile women hiding in plain sight, each with a less-than-stellar moral reputation. Rahab was a Canaanite prostitute who helped the Jewish spies when they were scouting out the Promised Land.[2] Ruth was a Moabite, and Moabites could not "enter the LORD's assembly; none of their descendants, even to the tenth generation, may ever enter the LORD's assembly" (Deuteronomy 23:3). Tamar, a Canaanite, was the daughter-in-law of Judah. She disguised herself as a prostitute and was impregnated by him.[3] And Bathsheba, the wife of Uriah the Hittite, was the Gentile woman King David committed adultery with.[4]

What do we learn from these four Gentile women in the line of King Jesus? First, God always keeps his promises. He promised Abraham a transethnic family, and he delivered it through Jesus.[5]

Second, no one is too broken that God can't repair, restore, and adopt them into his colorful family. Regardless of one's ethnicity, regardless of one's maleness or femaleness, Jesus has swung open the gates to his Father's Kingdom. All who enter, enter by grace alone. All who join the family are marked by faith in the crucified and risen Messiah.

With Christ's birth, the promise God made to Abraham was being fulfilled—salvation for all peoples who follow him. However, not everyone was as pleased as Simeon to hear this.

Hometown Prejudice

From the very beginning of Jesus' public ministry, he rocked the boat of cultural expectation.

Just as he had done as a little boy growing up in Nazareth, Jesus went to his hometown synagogue on the Sabbath. On this day, he stood up and read from the scroll of the prophet Isaiah:

The Spirit of the Lord is on me,
because he has anointed me
to preach good news to the poor.
He has sent me
to proclaim release to the captives

and recovery of sight to the blind,
to set free the oppressed,
to proclaim the year of the Lord's favor.

LUKE 4:18-19

After Jesus read these words, all eyes were glued to him. But then he said the unthinkable—"Today as you listen, this Scripture has been fulfilled" (Luke 4:21). Could he really be the long-awaited Jewish Messiah? Could he be the one who would deliver the Jewish people from Roman injustice and oppression? Had the King of the Jews finally answered their prayers?

Jesus' hometown synagogue spoke well of his sermon at first, but then the mood shifted dramatically and dangerously.

In reading the words of the prophet Isaiah, Jesus revealed what was always true about God's promised Messiah: he would be the Savior and unifier of both Jews *and* Gentiles, incorporating them in the family God promised to Abraham. In reading this passage from Isaiah 61, Jesus stopped short of announcing judgment on Gentiles, ending the quotation with "to proclaim the year of the LORD's favor" and omitting "and the day of our God's vengeance" (Isaiah 61:2). Bible scholar N. T. Wright comments,

> The passage [Jesus] quotes is about the Messiah. . . . But, though this text goes on to speak of vengeance on evildoers, Jesus doesn't quote that bit. Instead, he seems to have drawn on the larger picture in Isaiah

and elsewhere which speaks of Israel being called to
be the light to the nations. . . . The servant-Messiah
has not come to inflict punishment on the nations,
but to bring God's love and mercy to them.[6]

When those in attendance began to dismiss Jesus as just
"Joseph's son" (Luke 4:22), Jesus reminded them about the
Jewish prophets Elijah and Elisha, whom God used in miraculous ways—on behalf of Gentiles. In fact, in these stories, there
were no miracles for the Jews, who rejected these prophets, but
only for Gentiles: the widow in Sidon and Naaman the Syrian.

What was Jesus' hometown's response to this information?

When they heard this, everyone in the synagogue was
enraged. They got up, drove him out of town, and
brought him to the edge of the hill that their town was
built on, intending to hurl him over the cliff. But he
passed right through the crowd and went on his way.

LUKE 4:28-30

Why would they behave in this extreme way?

Jesus' hometown synagogue was waiting for the Jewish
Messiah to make Israel great again. But Jesus, the true
Messiah, came to be a great Savior and unifier of *all* God's
people. God did not have only a Jewish family but a big,
transcultural family of diversity, equality, and oneness.

Jesus' sermon was not well received even though it was
gospel truth.

When you and I leverage our lives to heal the racial divide through the gospel, some people may try to throw us off a cliff too.

But Jesus hates the sin of racism; so should we.

Jesus came to unite the divided people of God; so should we.

Jesus leveraged his life for this gospel cause; so should we.

Jesus and the Seven-Hundred-Year Feud

Lurking beneath the surface in every ethnic group, there is an unwritten rule about another group of people that history, for whatever reason, says you are not supposed to love. There is always an "us" and a "them."

In Nigeria, the Igbo and Hausa tribes have ethnic tension, riddled with suspicion. The Rwandan genocide was due to Hutu and Tutsi tribal fighting. The Yugoslav wars were among Croatians, Serbians, and Slovenians. Today, in the Middle East, the Kurdish people are at war with many other groups in four separate countries based on centuries-old hurts and modern maps.

Our world is riddled with ethnic conflict. This great darkness has led to some of the world's greatest tragedies, from the transatlantic slave trade to the Holocaust. May we never be so quick to dismiss the past. If we do, it is at our own peril because we miss how we got to where we are.

The Bible tells us of one such ethnic conflict, and Jesus' response, in John 4.

One day Jesus told his Jewish disciples that "he had to

travel through Samaria" (John 4:4). Jesus' disciples would have found this absurd, dangerous, and blasphemous.

It was absurd because Jews did not travel through Samaria—it was inhabited by Samaritans.

It was dangerous because Samaritans might have killed Jesus and his Jewish disciples, or at least have given them a good thrashing for coming to their side of the tracks.

It was blasphemous because Samaritans were considered half-breeds and religious heretics. Samaritans were an ethnic mixture of Gentile and Jew, "resulting from the resettlement policies of the Assyrian exile of the northern ten tribes" in 722 BC.[7] And in AD 6, a group of Samaritans desecrated the Jewish Temple, widening the chasm between Samaritans and Jews even further. The ancient historian Josephus wrote,

> As Coponius, who we told you was sent along with Cyrenius, was exercising his office of procurator, and governing Judea, the following accidents happened. As the Jews were celebrating the feast of unleavened bread, which we call the Passover, it was customary for the priests to open the temple gates just after midnight. . . . When, therefore, those gates were first opened, some of the Samaritans came privately into Jerusalem, and threw about dead men's bodies in the cloisters; on which account the Jews afterward excluded them out of the temple, which they had not used to do at such festivals.[8]

JESUS THE BARRIER BREAKER AND FAMILY MAKER

By the time of Jesus, Jews and Samaritans had a seven-hundred-year history of hatred and prejudice. The division was ethnic *and* religious, because in antiquity, a person's ethnicity was united to their religious practice.[9] For example, being a Jew was defined not by a person's skin color but by their religious practices (Torah observance, food laws, circumcision).

Jesus was born into a culture that had hundreds of years of past prejudice that was creating problems in the present. The unhealed wounds of past divisions were bleeding on Jesus, his disciples, and the Samaritans. This is why Jesus "had to travel through Samaria."

WE ALL DRINK FROM THE SAME JAR

As Jesus was traveling through this "forbidden" area, he encountered a Samaritan woman. She had arrived at Jacob's Well at noon, the hottest time of day. Most women collected water in the cool of the morning or in the evening, but this woman appeared to be avoiding people. She had had five husbands, and she was currently living with a man who was not her husband. Both in Jewish and Samaritan cultures, her behavior would have been scandalous.

The Samaritan woman is often viewed as an immoral person, but most likely she was a victim of men who used her and threw her away. If she had committed adultery, she could have been stoned to death. She was probably living with the man who was not her husband because she needed a way to survive.

Jesus asked this woman for a drink. She was shocked—both because he was a Jew and because he was a man. The Pharisees and many of the Jews would have considered both her and her water jar unclean because she was a Samaritan.[10] Furthermore, the Jewish Messiah was also breaking a *gender* barrier. Rabbis did not talk to women in public.

As this scandalous conversation continued, Jesus revealed that he is the spring of living water that leads to eternal life: "Everyone who drinks from this water will get thirsty again. But whoever drinks from the water that I will give him will never get thirsty again. In fact, the water I will give him will become a well of water springing up in him for eternal life" (John 4:13-14).

Eternal life speaks of sharing and participating in the life of the triune God forever.

Eternal life speaks of resurrection from the dead in the new heaven and new earth.

Eternal life speaks of forgiveness of sins, becoming a new creation, and being reconciled to Jesus' Father.

Eternal life speaks of being declared the righteousness of Christ and of becoming the Spirit's dwelling place.

Eternal life speaks of being adopted into God's multiethnic family of reconciliation.

Eternal life speaks of Jesus defeating sin, death, and evil.

Eternal life speaks of racism being crucified at the altar of Jesus' blood-soaked cross.

The words of the prophet Isaiah echo in Jesus' revelation that he is a spring of living water, the promised Messiah:

Come, everyone who is thirsty,
come to the water;
and you without silver,
come, buy, and eat! . . .
You will summon a nation [*goyim*]
    you do not know,
and nations who do not know you
    will run to you.
For the LORD your God,
even the Holy One of Israel,
has glorified you.

ISAIAH 55:1, 5

Everyone—Jew, White, Black, Asian, Latino, Indigenous: all are welcome to drink from the Living Water himself. At Jesus' fountain of living water, there are no separate water fountains for God's people; regardless of our ethnicities, we all drink at the same well of grace. In our dry and weary land of racial division, Jesus provides living water that reconciles us to him and to each other so we can live in harmony.

THE STORY WITHIN THE STORY

After Jesus declared that he is the source of living water, the conversation twisted and turned through the woman's scandalous past, through current ethnic disputes, and finally to the Samaritan woman's statement, "When [the Messiah] comes, he will explain everything to us" (John 4:25).

Jesus' response was momentous: "I, the one speaking to you, am he" (John 4:26).

In several Gospel passages, we see Jesus specifically forbidding people and demons to speak of his identity.[11] But here he is forthright about who he is.

Of all the people Jesus could have revealed his identity to, he chose a Samaritan woman during a seven-hundred-year-old racial feud.

Jesus is trying to tell us something.

He is a barrier breaker, a family maker. God's family is one, united in Christ, sealed by the Spirit's presence.

When Jesus revealed to the woman that he is the Messiah, she left her water at the well and ran back to tell the Samaritan people the Messiah had come. Eventually, the Samaritans from the city of Sychar believed in Jesus. They even asked him to stay longer. The disciples were in shock, but Jesus told them, "Look around! You just left a city full of Samaritans, but you did not tell them. The harvest is ready!"[12] I suspect they did not tell the Samaritans about the Messiah because seven hundred years of ethnocentrism clouded their vision.

The Samaritan woman is the first person to whom Jesus revealed that he is the Messiah. She is also one of the first missionaries of the gospel.

What is a Samaritan? A Samaritan is a Jew and a Gentile in one body.

What is the church? Jews and Gentiles (Whites, Blacks, Latinos, Asians, and others) in one body:

> We were all baptized by one Spirit into one body—
> whether Jews or Greeks, whether slaves or free—and
> we were all given one Spirit to drink.
>
> 1 CORINTHIANS 12:13

> He made peace between Jews and Gentiles by
> creating in himself one new people from the two
> groups. Together as one body, Christ reconciled both
> groups to God by means of his death on the cross,
> and our hostility toward each other was put to death.
>
> EPHESIANS 2:15-16, NLT

What did the Samaritan woman do when she found out that Jesus was the Messiah? She became a missionary.

What is the church to do? Jesus' church is a multiethnic bride that is on mission to tell others that Jesus is the source of living water that springs up to eternal life. *All* are welcome to come and freely drink.

Jesus is a barrier breaker, a family maker.

The Roman Centurion

After Jesus preached in his hometown synagogue, the people of Nazareth wanted to throw him off a cliff for saying that the Messiah came to include both Jews and Gentiles in God's family.

Wisely, Jesus and his disciples packed up their belongings and relocated to the city of Capernaum as their new headquarters. While in that city, a Roman centurion, a man with great authority who participated in Rome's violent occupation and oppression of Israel, asked Jesus to heal his servant.

Jesus responded, "Am I to come and heal him?" (Matthew 8:7). In Jesus' time, Roman centurions were despised by Jews. They were considered unclean, ungodly, and untrustworthy. Jesus asked the centurion if he was to come to his house, because it would have been scandalous for a Jewish rabbi to enter the home of a Gentile military leader that oppressed Israel. Jews were accustomed to the injustice of Romans crucifying Jewish men on crosses that lined the streets of ancient Israel. Death by crucifixion was so heinous that the law forbade Roman citizens being crucified.

But right in the middle of this mess, something beautiful happened. The centurion told Jesus,

> Lord . . . I am not worthy to have you come under
> my roof. But just say the word, and my servant will
> be healed. For I too am a man under authority,
> having soldiers under my command. I say to this
> one, "Go," and he goes; and to another, "Come,"
> and he comes; and to my servant, "Do this!" and
> he does it.
>
> MATTHEW 8:8-9

The centurion recognized in Jesus one who had authority over the spiritual realm in the same way he commanded his troops. And Jesus, in turn, marveled at a Gentile's faith: "Hearing this, Jesus was amazed and said to those following him, 'Truly I tell you, I have not found anyone in Israel with so great a faith. I tell you that many will come from east and west to share the banquet with Abraham, Isaac, and Jacob in the kingdom of heaven'" (Matthew 8:10-11).

It is ironic that in Jesus' hometown synagogue he was rejected because he advocated to include Gentiles in the family of God, which is exactly what God promised Abraham he would do. Yet he was trusted and honored by this Gentile Roman oppressor of the Jewish people.

Jesus came to free the oppressed *and* the oppressor. In this text, we see that God's banquet is a table of grace. Regardless of one's ethnic or social status, all who call on the name of Jesus will be saved from sin and death and are welcome at Abraham's diverse table. All who call on the name of Jesus are invited into his Kingdom. God's Kingdom is a multinational kaleidoscope of siblings. If Jesus welcomes all who trust in him, shouldn't we?

The Canaanite Woman

In another situation, Jesus breaks down racial barriers, showing us how to demonstrate love to others in a racially toxic culture.

The Messiah and his disciples were journeying through the Phoenician coastal towns of Tyre and Sidon. In the Old Testament, this Canaanite area was associated with idolatrous Baal worship and evil acts that accompanied appeasing this deity. The Canaanites were enemies of Israel. In this story, once again, we see Jesus interacting with Gentiles within the Promised Land, breaking down the racial barriers of his day, just as we are called to do in our time.

In Tyre and Sidon, Jesus encountered a Canaanite (Syro-Phoenician) woman who cried out for the Jewish Messiah to heal her demon-possessed daughter.

She fell at Jesus' feet as a sign of faith in him. She believed he had the power to heal her daughter, even calling him the Son of David (a messianic title). Often in times of desperation, we do not care what ethnicity a person is—we just want help. The Jewish disciples tried to get rid of the Gentile woman, but she would have none of that. She had a persistent faith in the Son of David. She loved her daughter and wanted her child healed.

The Canaanite woman and Jesus had a dialogue that seems troublesome on the surface:

[Jesus] replied, "I was sent only to the lost sheep of the house of Israel."

But she came, knelt before him, and said, "Lord, help me!"

He answered, "It isn't right to take the children's bread and throw it to the dogs."

"Yes, Lord," she said, "yet even the dogs eat the crumbs that fall from their masters' table."

Then Jesus replied to her, "Woman, your faith is

great. Let it be done for you as you want." And from that moment her daughter was healed.

MATTHEW 15:24-28

In this exchange, it's like Jesus was saying, "Gentile woman, you know many of my Jewish kindred consider you a dog, right? Are you sure you want to ask me—a Jewish rabbi—to heal your daughter?" Jesus was referencing the racial division between Jews and Gentiles. Many Jews considered Gentiles dogs. Jesus told the woman that he was sent on a mission to reveal himself as the promised Messiah to the children of Israel first.

However, Jesus' saying this does not negate how Jesus interacted with Gentiles within the geographical boundaries of the Promised Land. As the apostle Paul wrote, "I am not ashamed of this Good News about Christ. It is the power of God at work, saving everyone who believes—the Jew *first* and also the Gentile" (Romans 1:16, NLT, emphasis added). In this statement, Paul is following Jesus' model of building Abraham's family.

As Jesus delivered the woman's daughter of demonic possession, he helped his Jewish disciples and those bearing witness to his power and love to overcome their prejudices against Gentiles as well.

The Good Samaritan

In another familiar story, Jesus reveals the sacrifices required to love others in a world where it is easier to stay "us" and "them." It begins with Jesus in conversation with a Jewish religious scholar who was attempting to catch him in a trap:

> Then an expert in the law stood up to test him, saying, "Teacher, what must I do to inherit eternal life?"
>
> "What is written in the law?" he asked him. "How do you read it?"
>
> He answered, "Love the Lord your God with all your heart, with all your soul, with all your strength, and with all your mind," and "your neighbor as yourself."
>
> "You've answered correctly," he told him. "Do this and you will live."
>
> LUKE 10:25-28

Jesus told the religious scholar, "Do this and you will *live*." The word *live* is from the Greek *záō*. The kind of life Jesus describes is God's eternal kind of life. This kind of life cannot be achieved; it can only be received by faith as God's gift. The life God calls us to is a life of loving God, self, and neighbor.

But the Jewish religious leader, "wanting to justify himself," asked Jesus, "And who is my neighbor?" (Luke 10:29).

In his Jewish cultural context, his neighbor would have been only Jewish because of the historical ethnic conflict and distrust that existed between Jews and Gentiles. However, Jesus, the master teacher and the one who came to show humanity a new, truer way to be human, launched into a story:

Jesus took up the question and said, "A man was going down from Jerusalem to Jericho and fell into the hands of robbers. They stripped him, beat him up, and fled, leaving him half dead. A priest happened to be going down that road. When he saw him, he passed by on the other side. In the same way, a Levite, when he arrived at the place and saw him, passed by on the other side."

LUKE 10:30-32

From Jerusalem to Jericho was a seventeen-mile trip with a three-thousand-foot descent. The road was winding and treacherous. Along this path were many places where robbers could hide, waiting to ambush unsuspecting travelers. Jerome, an early church father, described this road as "the bloody way" because of the violence that often took place on it.[13]

Jesus tells us that a man was robbed, beaten, and left for dead. He was laid out on the side of the road in a pool of blood. We know the man was Jewish because Jesus does not identify him as a Gentile to his Jewish listeners. Then Jesus says a Jewish priest and a Levite, both coming from Jerusalem, saw their bloody kinsman. They walked by him on the other side of the road, neglecting his need, moving past his pain. While some might suggest there was a purification reason for their actions, in fact, there was no fear of becoming unclean from touching a dead person, because they had just completed their religious duties in Jerusalem—they were heading "down," to Jericho.

The Temple, where the priest and Levite served, was the place where God's space and people's space overlapped into one. It was a place of worship. Yet the two religious leaders walked past the man in need. Never forget—the greatest act of worship is loving your neighbor because you love God; the two go together. Listeners would have expected that the priest and Levite would be examples of loving their neighbor, but Jesus flipped the script:

> But a Samaritan on his journey came up to him,
> and when he saw the man, he had compassion. He
> went over to him and bandaged his wounds, pouring
> on olive oil and wine. Then he put him on his own
> animal, brought him to an inn, and took care of
> him. The next day he took out two denarii, gave
> them to the innkeeper, and said, "Take care of him.
> When I come back I'll reimburse you for whatever
> extra you spend."
>
> LUKE 10:33-35

Given the religious and ethnic division between Jews and Samaritans, the thought that a Samaritan would stop and help a Jew was like saying, "Square circles"—it just didn't make sense. What's interesting is that Jesus said the Samaritan saw a "man"—not a Jew, but a man. You and I will not be able to love people beyond the label we attach to them. This fact is

why Scripture says, "Love your *neighbor* as you love yourself."
And as we see in this story, neighbor means everyone. Every
human bears the image of God and is worthy of love, respect,
and dignity. I do not have to agree with you to love you. Love
does not require agreement, just compassion.

When the Samaritan saw the Jewish man—bloody and
beaten—he had compassion for him. Compassion means
you are feeling the pain of another person as though you
were suffering yourself. The plight of the Jewish man became
the Samaritan man's plight. Love shares in suffering.

The Samaritan put bandages on the man's wounds. He
poured oil to keep the wounds soft and wine to keep them
from being infected. He then placed the man on his animal and put him up in an inn so the man could recover.
Helping the man who was supposed to be his ethnic enemy
was expensive. Everything he used to help him had a finan-
cial cost. The amount of money he paid the inn for the man
to recover from his injuries would have covered about a two-
month stay.[14]

There was another cost too. Imagine when the Samaritan
returned home and told his family and friends what he had
done for a Jew! I suspect he would have been called a "Jew
lover" or been told "#JewishLivesDoNotMatter" and asked,
"How could you help *him*?"

Loving your neighbor looks like giving mercy to the
"other." It looks like refusing to give in to historical racial
bigotry. It looks like saying, "I am not going to carry this sin

into my future. I am going to break the cycle of hate by being merciful to the 'other' now."

I suspect the Jewish audience overhearing Jesus share this story was silent in a holy hush. I imagine it was one of those moments where the presence of God was palpable. He then said,

> "Which of these three do you think proved to be a neighbor to the man who fell into the hands of the robbers?"
>
> "The one who showed mercy to him," he said.
>
> Then Jesus told him, "Go and do the same."

LUKE 10:36-37

We are born in a sin-saturated world. The demonic powers are running rampant. Racism, among other sins, is a foul odor that needs to be replaced by the fragrance of love. Go and be merciful to your neighbors of all ethnicities. In and through the power of the Messiah, we can heal the racial divide by seeing those who are different from us as our neighbors and then loving them as we love ourselves.

Abba's House Is Home for *All* People

Throughout his public ministry, Jesus continued to afflict the comfortable and comfort the afflicted. One experience made Jesus truly angry—keeping people from receiving his Father's salvation by turning his gospel into a moneymaking scheme.

This exploitation is what was happening at the Temple in Jerusalem, as told in Mark 11.

When Solomon had dedicated the first Temple, Gentiles were expected to come and worship the one true God.[15] The hope that Gentiles would come to Jerusalem and worship God alongside Jews is threaded throughout the writing of the prophet Isaiah.[16] By the time of Jesus, Gentiles were supposed to be able to pray in the outer courts of the Temple. On the Temple Mount, there was a series of courts getting nearer to the inner sanctum called the Holy of Holies. Those closer to God, such as the priests or Jewish men, were allowed nearer to this area. The Gentiles could come to the Temple to worship but were allowed only in the outermost area. However, in a tragic scene of spiritual abuse, systemic injustice, and prejudice, the Court of the Gentiles had been turned into a marketplace by profiteering Sadducees.

The Sadducees were an ancient Jewish sect that represented the party of the high priest, aristocratic families, and wealthy merchants. They owned commercial rights from Rome to choose who could buy and sell on the Mount of Olives and in the Court of the Gentiles.[17] In the preceding years, the Court of the Gentiles had become a religious moneymaking scam. The Temple had become, as Jesus called it, a "den of thieves" (Mark 11:17).

The Sadducees were intentionally cheating Jews and Gentiles by charging exorbitant prices to exchange their currency. They routinely disqualified the sacrificial animals brought from people's homes so people had to purchase expensive sacrificial animals from the merchants instead.[18] To Jesus, the Temple had the foul smell of systemic injustice, corruption, prejudice against Gentiles, and spiritual abuse. This is what made Jesus explode with righteous anger:

> He went into the temple and began to throw out those buying and selling. He overturned the tables of the money changers and the chairs of those selling doves, and would not permit anyone to carry goods through the temple. He was teaching them: "Is it not written, My house will be called a house of prayer for all nations [Isaiah 56:7]? But you have made it a den of thieves [Jeremiah 7:11]!"
>
> MARK 11:15-17

Jesus knew the purpose of the Temple was to draw and gather a multiethnic community of worshipers to his Abba. Jesus' vision of a house of prayer for all ethnicities is a precursor to the multiethnic congregations of the early church and a model for believers of different ethnic backgrounds to live in peace as a unifying presence in the world. This idea that Jesus echoes is from Isaiah:

> I will bring them to my holy mountain
> and let them rejoice in my house of prayer.
> Their burnt offerings and sacrifices
> will be acceptable on my altar,

for my house will be called a house of prayer
for all nations.

ISAIAH 56:7

After Jesus reacted to the corruption in the Temple and called out the exploitation, the chief priest and the scribes wanted to kill him.[19]

All Are Welcome at God's Table of Grace

This look at Jesus' ministry is by no means exhaustive. But as we've seen in looking at these passages, while Jesus is the Jewish Messiah, he spent a large portion of his ministry breaking down barriers and making good on God's promise to provide Abraham a multiethnic family.

Aside from these stories, the Gospel writers, led by God the Holy Spirit, consistently inform the original audience—and us—of the influence that Gentiles had on Jesus' life. Jesus was raised in Galilee, an area that reflected the ethnic diversity of the Roman Empire. Jesus grew up near "Assyrians, Babylonians, Egyptians, Macedonians, Persians, Romans, Syrians, and indigenous Canaanites."[20] The pervading Greek culture and the Roman economic and governmental administration would have shaped Jesus' life in Galilee.

Jesus was not exempt from the ethnic tensions that permeated his culture. Most likely while working with his earthly father, Joseph, in construction, he would have traveled to cities such as Sepphoris, Tiberias, and Caesarea Philippi. Galilee was also surrounded by Greek states and submerged in the Greek way of life.[21]

Because Jesus grew up in Galilee with Gentiles of various ethnicities and cultural practices, he would have been accustomed to the attitudes of Jewish supremacy over Gentiles and Gentile supremacy over Jews. For example, the Roman philosopher Cicero (106–43 BC) wrote, "As the Greeks say, all men are divided into two classes—Greeks and barbarians. The Greeks called any man a barbarian who could not speak Greek; and they despised him and put up the barriers against him."[22] Aristotle believed that non-Greeks, which would have included the Jewish people, were "barbarians belonging to the bestial class."[23] Livy, a Roman historian, wrote, "The Greeks wage a truceless war against people of other races, against barbarians."[24] Even Plato believed that barbarians were "our enemies by nature."[25] The ancient world of Jesus had high barriers that deeply divided Jews and Gentiles, and various Gentile groups also were divided against other Gentiles.

In God's providence, Jesus was nurtured in a context of ethnic diversity, prejudice, and injustice.

With Jesus' experiences, he fulfilled this messianic prophecy:

Land of Zebulun and land of Naphtali,
along the road by the sea, beyond the Jordan,
Galilee of the Gentiles.
The people who live in darkness

have seen a great light,
and for those living in the land of the shadow of death,
a light has dawned.

MATTHEW 4:15-16

It is in this world of division and "darkness" that Jesus performed his feeding miracles, where we'll close this chapter. We sometimes skip over the significance of these two accounts, as the stories the Gospel writers recount are very similar. But let's dig a little deeper. While the first feeding miracle is on the *Jewish* side of the lake, the second feeding miracle takes place in the Gentile, *Decapolis* area of the lake.[26] Mark's narrative of the two miraculous feedings—one for Jews and one for Gentiles—was not accidental or just a carbon copy. It acts as a living portrait of the anticipated messianic banquet that the prophet Isaiah foretold:

On this mountain,
the LORD of Armies will prepare for all the peoples a
    feast of choice meat,
a feast with aged wine, prime cuts of choice meat, fine
    vintage wine.
On this mountain
he will swallow up the burial shroud,
the shroud over all the peoples,
the sheet covering all the nations.
When he has swallowed up death once and for all,
the LORD God will wipe away the tears

from every face
and remove his people's disgrace
from the whole earth,
for the LORD has spoken.
ISAIAH 25:6-8

Jesus fed Jews and Gentiles who were separated by a lake but who would one day eat at the same table of grace and be unified as the new people of God: the church. There is more than enough room for Jews, Asians, Whites, Latinos, Blacks, Indigenous Peoples, and every other tribe and tongue "to share the banquet with Abraham, Isaac, and Jacob in the kingdom of heaven" (Matthew 8:11).

Miracles happen around food. Cultures are exchanged around a meal. Community is found around the Bread of Life, who shared his life with us so we could be in the Father's family.

Jesus, the Son of God, truly is the barrier breaker and family maker.

| | | | | **MARINATE ON THIS** | | | |

PRAYER

Father,
By grace through faith in your beloved Son,
I am now a member of the beautifully diverse family
*   that you promised Abraham.*
In your family, there is no favoritism.
We are equal in your sight, and we are your delight.

Lord Jesus,
Teach me to love like you do.
Teach me to see every person as an image-bearer of God,
*   worthy of love, respect, and dignity.*

Holy Spirit,
Give me the courage to cast aside prejudice and racial biases.
Give me the strength to confront evil in the world and
*   evil in myself.*
Give me power in this hour to heal our racial divide.
In Jesus' name,
Amen.

THINGS TO THINK ABOUT

- Jesus is the barrier breaker and the family maker, the fulfillment of God's promise to Abraham that he would be "the father of many nations" (Genesis 17:5).

- In reading the words of the prophet Isaiah to his hometown synagogue, Jesus revealed what was always true about God's promised Messiah: he would be the Savior and unifier of both Jews *and* Gentiles, incorporating them into the family God promised to Abraham.

- Jesus' vision of a house of prayer for all ethnicities is a precursor to the multiethnic congregations of the early church and a model for believers of different ethnic backgrounds to live in peace as a unifying presence in the world.

QUESTIONS TO DISCUSS

1. Do you have friends from different ethnic or cultural backgrounds than yours? How have these friendships enhanced your life?

2. Read Luke 4:16-19. What was the significance of Jesus reading these words from Isaiah in the synagogue? What does this story show us about Jesus' desire to heal our racial divide?

3. How did Jesus respond to people of other ethnicities in his ministry? List some traits. Do you see these traits in your own life? Explain.

GOSPEL BEHAVIORS TO PRACTICE

Make a consistent effort to eat dinner with people from different ethnicities in your home or their home. As I say at the end of the chapter, "Miracles happen around food."

CHAPTER 4

THE BIRTH OF GOD'S MULTIETHNIC FAMILY

As a pastor, I have had the honor of sitting at the bedside of people getting ready to transition from this life to the next. Watching someone die, especially one who has the peace of Jesus, is beautiful. There is sadness and deep joy all at once ricocheting in your soul.

An older White member of our church named Bob, who was known as a businessman with integrity and a flourishing faith, had been battling brain cancer. He was just about ready to graduate into the presence of Jesus. I sat quietly by this older saint's bed as he mustered enough strength to say, "Pastor, keep teaching the people to obey Jesus. Keep teaching the people to love God and to love their neighbors as they love themselves. Keep giving them gospel, Pastor. Teach the people to make disciples of all people."

I was Bob's first Black senior pastor. I treasured every single word Bob said to me.

A person's last words have special significance and are to be acted upon. After King Jesus accomplished his saving, redemptive work and before he returned to heaven, he gave some last words to his Jewish disciples:

> Jesus came near and said to them, "All authority
> has been given to me in heaven and on earth. Go,
> therefore, and make disciples of all nations, baptizing
> them in the name of the Father and of the Son and
> of the Holy Spirit, teaching them to observe
> everything I have commanded you. And remember,
> I am with you always, to the end of the age."
> MATTHEW 28:18-20

After Jesus' resurrection, he gave his Jewish disciples a cross-cultural, missional mandate that is commonly called the great commission. This command is for every follower of Jesus. Reflect on this: Jesus is the true and faithful Israel, and his twelve Jewish disciples, who correspond to the twelve tribes of Israel, are the leaders of the new people of God. They were commissioned for a mission that extended back to the call of Abraham.[1] Jesus himself, through his sinless life, atoning death on the cross, and resurrection, fulfilled God's promise of giving Abraham a multiethnic family:

Remember that Christ came as a servant to the Jews to show that God is true to the promises he made to their ancestors. He also came so that the Gentiles might give glory to God for his mercies to them. That is what the psalmist meant when he wrote:

"For this, I will praise you among the Gentiles;
 I will sing praises to your name."
ROMANS 15:8-9, NLT

Never forget: racial unity is God's idea.

Jesus commanded his Jewish apprentices to take the Good News to the Gentiles ("all nations"). This instruction would have been especially difficult for them. As we have learned, historically, Jews had suffered under the Gentiles: four hundred years of slavery in Egypt, captivity in Babylon, and their current Roman oppression. Think about how radical and revolutionary it was for Jesus to command his Jewish disciples, "Go share the gospel with those who have enslaved, killed, and oppressed your people. Teach them to obey and follow my way of the Kingdom." Only the love of God in Christ by the Spirit's power can break down the barriers that divide and destroy us. The depth of this call was so urgent that Jesus told his Jewish disciples, "You will receive power when the Holy Spirit has come on you, and you will be my witnesses in Jerusalem, in all Judea and Samaria, and to the ends of the earth" (Acts 1:8).

In this verse, Jesus gives a geographical outline of the book of Acts. The Jewish disciples are in Jerusalem in chapters 1–7 and in Judea and Samaria in chapters 8–12. Then they take the gospel to the ends of the earth in chapters 13–28.

But do not move too quickly. Sit with this for a moment: a ragamuffin group of poor Galilean Jews has their lives reimagined by Jesus' resurrection so much that they leave all they know to join Jesus on his mission of reconciling the world to his Father and to each other, forming the family promised to Abraham.

You are a participant in this redemption story. This is *your* story. This is *my* story. This is *God's* story. It is a story of love.

Tongues of Fire and a Spirit of Unity

Jerusalem was buzzing with excitement. Jews from all over the known world were in the City of David to celebrate the annual Jewish festival called the Feast of Weeks.[2] This feast was held fifty days (seven weeks) after Passover, which celebrated God freeing Israel from slavery in Egypt.

But there was another group of Jews who had a different reason to celebrate. The Messiah who had been crucified was now alive. After Jesus' life, death, and resurrection, there was a greater Passover, a greater deliverance. Jesus now set Jews and Gentiles free from slavery to sin and death. He saved them *from* slavery and *for* inclusion into his family. And now God the Holy Spirit, the promise of God the Father, was coming to take the Son's church global.

As the disciples were gathered, the power of the Holy

Spirit, like a mighty rushing wind, empowered the Jewish disciples to speak in the languages of sixteen different geographical areas and distinct ethnic groups: "Parthians, Medes, Elamites; those who live in Mesopotamia, in Judea and Cappadocia, Pontus and Asia, Phrygia and Pamphylia, Egypt and the parts of Libya near Cyrene; visitors from Rome (both Jews and converts), Cretans and Arabs" (Acts 2:9-11). The Parthians, Medes, Elamites, and residents of Mesopotamia were ethnic groups from the area where Abraham was called and where Israel and Judah had been exiled in Assyria and Babylon.[3]

These people were blown away to hear God's mighty acts in the Messiah in their native language from people who did not usually speak their language. Here is proof of the lengths God will go to in order to unify his family in Christ Jesus.

This scene recalls the story of the tower of Babel in Genesis 11, where the people of the world were scattered and divided by language due to their rebellion. The people could "not understand one another's speech" (Genesis 11:7). In Genesis 12, God promised to regather his scattered children through a covenant with Abraham, through whose family "all the peoples on earth will be blessed" (Genesis 12:3). And now, in Acts 2, at Pentecost in Jerusalem, the Spirit empowered the new people of God to overcome the sin of ethnic prejudice and division, and for the first time since Babel, language was no longer a barrier, as the people heard the disciples "declaring the magnificent acts of God in [their] own tongues" (Acts 2:11).

At this event, the apostle Peter appealed to the crowd to repent and be baptized to "receive the gift of the Holy Spirit. For the promise is for you and for your children, and for all who are far off, as many as the Lord our God will call" (Acts 2:38-39). All who call on the name of the Lord will be forgiven of their sins and included in the family promised to Abraham: "You are the sons of the prophets and of the covenant that God made with your ancestors, saying to Abraham, And all the families of the earth will be blessed through your offspring" (Acts 3:25).

Representation Matters

The first Christians walked in the power of the sin-forgiving, unifying, reconciling work of King Jesus.

At Pentecost, the family God promised to Abraham was born. Despite this epic move of God in increasing his family, there were growing pains: "There arose a complaint by the Hellenistic Jews against the Hebraic Jews that their widows were being overlooked in the daily distribution" (Acts 6:1).

The first Christians practiced providing for the poor and those in need, as the Bible commands.[4] Yet amid this beautiful act of grace, the Hebraic Jewish widows were being shown favoritism over the Hellenistic (Greek) Jewish widows. This conflict was overflowing with racial overtones. The Hebraic Jews were from Palestine and largely spoke Aramaic. They were thought to be purer Jews because they were closer to the Temple and lived in the Promised Land.

The Greek-influenced Jews outside of the Promised Land had adopted a lot of Greek culture. The Greek Jews took their complaint to the Hebraic Jewish apostles:

> The Twelve summoned the whole company of the
> disciples and said, "It would not be right for us
> to give up preaching the word of God to wait on
> tables. Brothers and sisters, select from among you
> seven men of good reputation, full of the Spirit and
> wisdom, whom we can appoint to this duty. But we
> will devote ourselves to prayer and to the ministry
> of the word." This proposal pleased the whole
> company. So they chose Stephen, a man full of faith
> and the Holy Spirit, and Philip, Prochorus, Nicanor,
> Timon, Parmenas, and Nicolaus, a convert from
> Antioch. They had them stand before the apostles,
> who prayed and laid their hands on them.
> ACTS 6:2-6

The first Christians, an ethnically mixed family, wisely chose seven Greek men to lead this effort. This solution was gospel innovation at its finest. Since the Hellenistic widows felt slighted, the Christians chose Hellenistic Jews to be in charge of the distribution. This has some powerful lessons for us today.

First, these Greek-influenced disciples were filled with gospel integrity. They were committed to Jesus, his Kingdom, and his truth, not to their ethnic group above another. Disciples are pro-Jesus, which makes them pro-human.

Second, the Greek men were able to represent the Greek people's needs and perspectives. Representation matters. The Greek men could advocate for and educate the Hebraic Jews about their Greek siblings. When you can talk to someone who understands you and who has walked in your shoes, it makes a difference. As disciples of Jesus, we must cultivate cross-cultural friendships, knowing they are vital to human development.

Third, by choosing seven Greek men, the leadership of the community was diversified. Sharing leadership influence across ethnic lines makes a huge difference. When people see people who look like them in positions of leadership, it helps them know that they matter and are not overlooked. Disciples understand that sharing leadership with people of color encourages those who feel unseen and undervalued.

Do you remember how Black people responded when the late Chadwick Boseman played Black Panther in Marvel's film franchise? This was the first time we saw a Black superhero in a starring role of this magnitude. Similarly, as a Black pastor who went from a poor, at-risk environment to now having a doctorate in New Testament, to being an author and leading Transformation Church, by God's grace, I inspire our youth who come from similar circumstances. Ethnic diversity in church leadership matters. When you see someone who looks like you, it encourages you.

The first Christians understood this principle, and they were proactive in healing a divide before it became a schism.

The Ethiopian Eunuch

The book of Acts reads like an action movie. Wonderful things were happening through the first Christians—healings, salvations, justice, baptism, and church growth. But the disciples initially stayed in Jerusalem—among Jews. Jesus was very specific in his words. He wanted them to go to the Samaritans, the people that the Jews were in a seven-hundred-year racial feud with. He also wanted them to go to other Gentiles, the people they considered unclean and who historically had oppressed them. The gospel calls us to break down barriers.

So how did God get the Jewish disciples to take the gospel out of Jerusalem to the Gentiles?

> A severe persecution broke out against the church in Jerusalem, and all except the apostles were scattered throughout the land of Judea and Samaria. Devout men buried Stephen [one of the Hellenistic Jews we just read about] and mourned deeply over him. Saul, however, was ravaging the church. He would enter house after house, drag off men and women, and put them in prison.
>
> ACTS 8:1-3

Persecution forced the Jewish disciples to move out of Jerusalem into Samaria, and they took the gospel with them. Philip finally proclaimed the Messiah to Samaritans, who came to faith in large numbers. As we can see, humanity matters to God. He promised Abraham a family made up of all the different ethnicities. He is a covenant maker and promise keeper. When Jesus walked out of that tomb, God was fulfilling his promise to gather this family.

Persecution scattered God's people on mission, and they went about "preaching the gospel in many villages of the Samaritans" (Acts 8:25). Philip was crushing it. He was preaching the gospel. God was using him to save sinners, heal racial trauma, and build the Kingdom. The work begun in Jesus' ministry was now being extended through the Holy Spirit in his disciples.

Then an angel of the Lord told Philip to "get up and go south to the road that goes down from Jerusalem to Gaza" (Acts 8:26). Philip obeyed, and there he found "an Ethiopian man, a eunuch and high official of Candace, queen of the Ethiopians, who was in charge of her entire treasury" (Acts 8:27).[5]

While on his way back to Ethiopia from Jerusalem, this man was sitting in his chariot and reading the prophet Isaiah but without understanding what he was reading.

The Spirit told Philip to join the African in his chariot, and Philip explained that the prophet Isaiah was speaking of Jesus in the words the eunuch read. As they traveled, the eunuch spotted some water and asked, "Look, there's water. What would keep me from being baptized?" (Acts 8:37). So Philip baptized him then and there. The gospel of King Jesus, through the Ethiopian eunuch, spread to Northern Africa, reaching the ends of the earth. Vince L. Bantu writes, "North Africa had been a Christian region from the New Testament period that profoundly shaped much of Christian life and thought."[6] Many of Christianity's greatest theologians—like Augustine—were African. Christianity is not a White man's religion. Messiah Jesus is the seed of Abraham who graciously calls all people into the multiethnic family of Abraham.

When Jesus met the Samaritan woman at the well, he told his disciples, "Don't you say, 'There are still four more months, and then comes the harvest'? Listen to what I'm telling you: Open your eyes and look at the fields, because they are ready for harvest" (John 4:35). As the disciples, mobilized by persecution, took the gospel to the Samaritans and beyond, the truth of Jesus' statement became clear.

It took persecution to get the first Christians to move from comfort in Jerusalem among themselves to being uncomfortable among the Samaritans. But once the gospel began its move from Jerusalem, to Judea, and then to Samaria, the ends of the earth weren't far behind.

Peter and Cornelius

In 2017, I was in Israel for my final doctoral class. One of our last stops was the city of Joppa, which is about thirty miles northwest of Jerusalem on the shores of the Mediterranean Sea. As our tour bus rolled into Joppa, my eyes were drawn to a statue of a big fish that symbolized the story of Jonah. Jonah was the Jewish prophet who didn't want to go to

Nineveh and preach against their evil. Nineveh, the capital city of the Assyrian Empire, was a symbol of military power. It had a reputation for violence, sexual immorality, and idolatry. God told Jonah to go to these Gentiles, but he refused. Jonah wanted the Gentiles to remain unrepentant and to stand under God's judgment. Jonah knew that the one true God was forgiving, gracious, kind, loving, and compassionate. He knew that if Nineveh repented, God would relent of his promised judgment. Instead of offering the hope of God to these people lost in their ways, Jonah tried to escape God's presence, boarding a ship in Joppa that was bound for Tarshish—as far away as he could go.

Jonah tried to escape by sea, but God caused a storm. His shipmates tossed him in the ocean to stop the storm, and a big fish swallowed him. For three days he had time to think about his life, his God, and his calling. In the belly of the big fish, Jonah cried out to the God of mercy, "I will sacrifice to you with a voice of thanksgiving. I will fulfill what I have vowed. Salvation belongs to the LORD" (Jonah 2:9). Jonah went to Nineveh and preached. Led by their king, the Ninevites repented of their evil ways, and God didn't bring about the promised punishment. Jonah did not love the Ninevites, but the living, loving God did.

Centuries later, there was another Jewish prophet in Joppa. His name was Peter, and he didn't want to take God's mercy to Gentiles either. Enter Cornelius: an Italian military leader in the Roman war machine. He and his family lived in Caesarea. They were "God-fearers," which meant they were Gentiles who embraced the God of Israel but did not undergo circumcision to become full converts. However, Cornelius was good to the Jews. One afternoon, Cornelius saw a vision of an angel, who told him, "Now send men to Joppa and call for Simon, who is also named Peter. He is lodging with Simon, a tanner, whose house is by the sea" (Acts 10:5-6). Cornelius sent two servants and a soldier to Joppa to fetch Peter.

Meanwhile, Peter was praying on the roof. As he prayed, he became hungry, and God showed him foods that Jewish people would have considered unclean. A voice said, "Get up, Peter; kill and eat" (Acts 10:13). Being a good Jew, Peter wanted to keep kosher, which was an ethnic badge of being Jewish. Peter said, "No, Lord! . . . For I have never eaten anything impure and ritually unclean" (Acts 10:14). But the voice responded, "What God has made clean, do not call impure" (Acts 10:15). This happened three times. Keep in mind that Jewish ethnic boundary markers such as circumcision, food laws, and Sabbath observance were among the ways that the people of God were distinguished from Gentiles. But now that the Messiah had come, the markers of God's multiethnic family were faith in the Messiah and baptism.[7]

While Peter was still puzzled about this vision, Cornelius's men showed up. They brought Peter with them to Caesarea to meet Cornelius, who had gathered his family and friends. And then something beautiful happened to Peter at Cornelius's house. In a sacred moment between a poor

Jewish fisherman and a powerful Gentile military leader, Peter became a gracist:[8]

> Peter told them, "You know it is against our laws for a Jewish man to enter a Gentile home like this or to associate with you. But God has shown me that I should no longer think of anyone as impure or unclean. . . . I see very clearly that God shows no favoritism. In every nation, he accepts those who fear him and do what is right. This is the message of Good News for the people of Israel—that there is peace with God through Jesus Christ, who is Lord of all."
>
> ACTS 10:28, 34-36, NLT

This is an epic moment in church history. The resurrection of Jesus brings a new creation right in the middle of the old. As Paul writes, "It doesn't matter whether we have been circumcised or not. What counts is whether we have been transformed into a new creation. May God's peace and mercy be upon all who live by this principle; they are the new people of God" (Galatians 6:15-16, NLT).

When this group of Gentiles heard Peter's message about Jesus, they believed, and the Holy Spirit empowered the Gentiles to praise God in other languages they did not know, just as he had the Jewish believers at Pentecost. This was to affirm that the Gentiles were included in Abraham's family just as much as Jews were. Even though Cornelius and his family and friends did not bear the ethnic marks of being Jewish, they received the same Holy Spirit.

God the Holy Spirit is the source of power that incorporates us into the multiethnic body of Messiah Jesus. The Holy Spirit is the source of unity across our ethnic differences through "the bond of peace" (Ephesians 4:3), which is Jesus himself. The first chapters of Acts show how a homogeneous Jewish movement shifted to include the Samaritans, an African, and later an Italian. Gospel-shaped, Jesus-centered racial reconciliation is in our DNA.

From the very beginning of Christianity, the Jesus movement has been a multiethnic, global family. It is time for us to walk in step with gospel reconciliation to live out our purpose as the family of God.

| | | | **MARINATE ON THIS** | | | |

PRAYER

Father,
From the call of Abraham to the incarnation of the Messiah,
the calling of the Twelve, the Cross, and the Resurrection,
you have longed to create a forgiven, redeemed, diverse,
    unified family.

Lord Jesus,
Racial reconciliation matters to you.
You did not simply forgive us so we could stay racist but
    to make us gracist.
Your resurrection power is enough to break barriers and
    mend our hearts together.

Holy Spirit,
You are the unifier.
You are the source of power that unifies us.
I pray as Jonah prayed:
"But as for me, I will sacrifice to you with a voice of
    thanksgiving. I will fulfill what I have vowed.
    Salvation belongs to the LORD."
In Jesus' name,
Amen.

THINGS TO THINK ABOUT

- A ragamuffin group of poor Galilean Jews had their lives reimagined by Jesus' resurrection—so much so that they left all they knew to join Jesus on his mission of reconciling the world to his Father and to each other, forming the family promised to Abraham. You are a participant in this redemption story. This is *your* story. This is *my* story. This is *God's* story. It is a story of love.

- Representation matters. When you can talk to someone who understands you and who has walked in your shoes, it makes a difference. As disciples of Jesus, we must cultivate cross-cultural friendships, knowing they are vital to human development.

- God the Holy Spirit is the source of power that incorporates us into the multiethnic body of Messiah Jesus. The Holy Spirit is the source of unity across our ethnic differences through "the bond of peace" (Ephesians 4:3), which is Jesus himself.

QUESTIONS TO DISCUSS

1. When the Greek widows felt slighted in the food distribution, the apostles appointed Greek Jews to handle the food distribution going forward. Why does representation in leadership matter? What might this gospel ingenuity look like in our own time?

2. The church moved to spread the gospel beyond Jerusalem once "a severe persecution broke out." How do times of difficulty embolden gospel action? In the difficult work of healing our racial divide, what bold gospel actions will you take?

3. Jonah and Peter were both reluctant to preach to another ethnic group. What barriers did they see that divided them? What barriers divide ethnicities in the church today? How has Jesus the Messiah removed these barriers?

GOSPEL BEHAVIORS TO PRACTICE

1. Look for intentional ways to build cross-cultural friendships, where you seek to learn from your siblings of different ethnicities.

2. Interpret God's story through the Bible itself, not conservative or liberal political categories.

CHAPTER 5

PAUL AND
THE EARLY CHURCH

How does a zealous, Pharisaic Jewish nationalist who persecuted followers of Jesus become the lead apostle of Jesus, building Jesus' multiethnic, reconciled family? How does one suffer so deeply for something he once hated so strongly?

Consider these passages about Paul's past and his trials for the sake of the gospel:

> I was circumcised when I was eight days old. I am a pure-blooded citizen of Israel and a member of the tribe of Benjamin—a real Hebrew if there ever was one! I was a member of the Pharisees, who demand the strictest obedience to the Jewish law. I was so

zealous that I harshly persecuted the church. And as for righteousness, I obeyed the law without fault.

PHILIPPIANS 3:5-6, NLT

Five different times the Jewish leaders gave me thirty-nine lashes. Three times I was beaten with rods. Once I was stoned. Three times I was shipwrecked. Once I spent a whole night and a day adrift at sea. I have traveled on many long journeys. I have faced danger from rivers and from robbers. I have faced danger from my own people, the Jews, as well as from the Gentiles. I have faced danger in the cities, in the deserts, and on the seas. And I have faced danger from men who claim to be believers but are not. I have worked hard and long, enduring many sleepless nights. I have been hungry and thirsty and have often gone without food. I have shivered in the cold, without enough clothing to keep me warm.

Then, besides all this, I have the daily burden of my concern for all the churches.

2 CORINTHIANS 11:24-28, NLT

"[Jesus] said to me, 'Go, because I will send you far away to the Gentiles.'" [The crowd] listened to [Paul] up to this point. Then they raised their voices, shouting, "Wipe this man off the face of the earth! He should not be allowed to live!"

ACTS 22:21-22

When Paul met the risen Messiah on the road to Damascus, he was transformed from a persecutor of Jesus' church into an apostle of Jesus Christ. When he met Jesus, not only did he recognize that Jesus was the God of his ancestors in human flesh; he knew Jesus as the new and better Passover Lamb who set the captives free from sin, death, and evil. He knew Jesus was the new and better eternal Day of Atonement, who declares those who trust him by faith to be righteous, forgiven, clean, holy, and pure. He knew that Jesus was the head of a new race made up of all the diverse people groups, fulfilling God's promise to Abraham. He knew Jesus to be leading a new and better Exodus through a new and better covenant. He knew the people of God were now an interethnic, culturally diverse family, where God himself would dwell.[1]

When Paul met Jesus, scales fell from his eyes. He saw the bigger, better story of God's salvation in the Messiah. He now knew that the unsearchable riches of Christ united those who were divided, bringing those who were near (Jews) and those who were far away (Gentiles) together in the Messiah.[2]

My heart's cry is for you and me to join Jesus, Paul, and the early church in discovering the immensity of our salvation. It is time for us to embrace the reality that Jesus' sinless life, atoning death on the cross, and resurrection are not separate from God's promise to Abraham but the fulfillment of that promise. This truth is why we "accept each other just as Christ has accepted you so that God will be given glory. Remember that Christ came as a servant to the Jews to show that God is true to the promises he made to their ancestors. He also came so that the Gentiles might give glory to God for his mercies to them" (Romans 15:7-9, NLT).

God is a Father who desires for his children to love him and each other through the Son and by the Holy Spirit's power.

God Recycles

Our God does not waste anything—the good, the bad, or the ugly. He doesn't squander the people, places, and predicaments of our lives. Our Father in heaven, through the beautiful mystery of his loving providence, uses our backgrounds, culture, and life experiences as a canvas to recreate us into his ambassadors of reconciliation.[3]

Church tradition tells us that Paul's family was from Gischala, a Galilean village twelve miles northwest of Capernaum. The Romans conquered the area, likely making Paul's dad a slave and moving him to Tarsus. Paul's father faithfully observed the Torah in Tarsus. Eventually, he was freed from slavery and became a Roman citizen. Around AD 1, in the multicultural world of the eastern Mediterranean, Paul, the future racial reconciler and Jew-Gentile unifier, was born. Tarsus was a leading city in the epicenter of Turkey (in Cilicia). Paul's hometown was a source of philosophy, politics, industry, and culture. It was "the Harvard of the Roman Empire."[4] Tarsus had a flourishing textile business, which most likely would have been the basis of Paul's family business, tentmaking. Paul's father would have mentored him in the family trade. Because Paul grew up in a multilingual, multicultural city as a tentmaker, he would have interacted with Gentiles and understood Hellenistic (Greek) culture. His experience would have prepared him for his ministry as the apostle to the Gentiles (and the Jews).

Paul's multicultural upbringing became a strength in bridging the divide between Jews and Gentiles.

In Jerusalem, Paul was educated in the Torah by the great Pharisee teacher Gamaliel. It was Gamaliel who spoke wise words to the Jewish high council as the early church in Jerusalem began to gain momentum, advising them to let the movement run its course lest they find themselves fighting against God.[5]

Later, as an angry Jewish mob stoned Stephen (the first Christian martyr), the participants laid their garments at the feet of Paul (whose Jewish name was Saul), and "Saul agreed with putting him to death" (Acts 8:1). Paul's zeal for the Torah and his sect of Pharisaic Judaism led him to Damascus:

> Now Saul was still breathing threats and murder against the disciples of the Lord. He went to the high priest and requested letters from him to the synagogues in Damascus, so that if he found any men or women who belonged to the Way, he might bring them as prisoners to Jerusalem. As he traveled and was nearing Damascus, a light from heaven suddenly flashed around him. Falling to the ground,

he heard a voice saying to him, "Saul, Saul, why are you persecuting me?"

"Who are you, Lord?" Saul said.

"I am Jesus, the one you are persecuting," he replied. "But get up and go into the city, and you will be told what you must do."

ACTS 9:1-6

After Paul's encounter with the risen Messiah, his eyes were opened, and he was filled with God the Holy Spirit. He was never the same. He was born again, and he became a participant in God's new creation and mission. The remainder of his life would be poured out fiercely fighting to get Jews and Gentiles to be the new people of God through the saving work of Jesus, giving his Father the family that was promised Abraham. Paul wrote to the church in Rome,

> Abraham is the spiritual father of those who have faith but have not been circumcised. They are counted as righteous because of their faith. And Abraham is also the spiritual father of those who have been circumcised, but only if they have the same kind of faith Abraham had before he was circumcised. . . . For Abraham is the father of all who believe. That is what the Scriptures mean when God told him, "I have made you the father of many nations." This happened because Abraham believed in the God who brings the

dead back to life and who creates new things out
of nothing.

ROMANS 4:11-12, 16-17, NLT

Once Jesus and his vision for humanity took hold of him,
Paul's zealousness was unleashed on behalf of Jesus through
the Spirit's power, and nothing and no one was going to stop
him from preaching, "This is God's plan: Both Gentiles and
Jews who believe the Good News share equally in the riches
inherited by God's children. Both are part of the same body,
and both enjoy the promise of blessings because they belong
to Christ Jesus" (Ephesians 3:6, NLT).

Not even the apostle Peter.

Paul and Peter in Antioch

The city of Antioch is important in the story of Christianity.
The city was founded by Seleucus I, one of Alexander the
Great's generals and successors, and originally segregated
into two sectors—one for Syrians and one for Greeks. It was
settled by "retired soldiers from Seleucus's Macedonian army,
Cretans, Cypriotes, Argives, and Herakleidae . . . , Athenians
from Atigonia, Jews from nearby Palestine (some of whom
had served as mercenaries in Seleucus's army), native Syrians,
and a number of slaves of diverse origins."[6] Later, Antioch
was fractured into numerous ethnic ghettos. The population
was divided into eighteen tribes throughout the city. Because
of the ethnic divisions and influx of newcomers, Antioch

was prone to ethnic riots, like most Greco-Roman cities of this era.[7]

Despite the incredible ethnic division, Jesus' multiethnic church was established and flourished in Antioch. According to the book of Acts, "The disciples were first called Christians at Antioch" (11:26). As we have seen, in the ancient world, a person's ethnicity was tied to their religious practices.[8] The Gentiles were no longer considered pagans, and the Jews were now following the resurrected Messiah as their Lord. This mosaic of humanity was called "Christian" because they were no longer what they were before; they were a new ethnic group based on their new and united faith. Our salvation and unity across ethnic lines is the overflow of Jesus' saving work in fulfillment of God's covenant with Abraham.

It is important to note that the multiethnic church in Antioch was initiated by some courageous Hellenistic Jewish believers from Cyprus and Cyrene (in modern Libya):

> The believers who had been scattered during the
> persecution after Stephen's death traveled as far
> as Phoenicia, Cyprus, and Antioch of Syria. They
> preached the word of God, but only to Jews.
> However, some of the believers who went to Antioch
> from Cyprus and Cyrene began preaching to the
> Gentiles about the Lord Jesus. The power of the
> Lord was with them, and a large number of these
> Gentiles believed and turned to the Lord.
>
> ACTS 11:19-21, NLT

They decided that Jesus' fulfilling the Abrahamic covenant was more important than Jewish ethnocentrism.

The church in Jerusalem sent Barnabas to Antioch to see what was happening, and then Barnabas went to find Paul in Tarsus. Barnabas brought Paul to Antioch so he could experience this vibrant new Jesus community, where racial reconciliation through the Good News was flourishing. Barnabas knew that Paul was uniquely suited for working in a mixed ethnic context because of his multicultural upbringing, his passion for the gospel, and his theological expertise.

But then the harmony of the gospel was disrupted by the apostle Peter. Paul describes the encounter in his letter to the Galatians:

> When Peter came to Antioch, I had to oppose him
> to his face, for what he did was very wrong. When
> he first arrived, he ate with the Gentile believers,
> who were not circumcised. But afterward, when
> some friends of James came, Peter wouldn't eat with
> the Gentiles anymore. He was afraid of criticism
> from these people who insisted on the necessity
> of circumcision. As a result, other Jewish believers
> followed Peter's hypocrisy, and even Barnabas was
> led astray by their hypocrisy.
>
> GALATIANS 2:11-13, NLT

Paul opposed Peter because Peter ate with Gentiles until "some friends of James"—one of the leaders of the church in Jerusalem—arrived. Then Peter stopped eating with the Gentiles. Peter knew the Jewish believers from James didn't consider the Gentiles full members of God's family because they hadn't taken on the ethnic badges of being Jewish (i.e., circumcision). The irony was that in Jerusalem, James, John, and Peter had told Paul and Barnabas to "keep preaching to the Gentiles" (Galatians 2:9, NLT).

Why did Peter turn his back on Jesus, his gospel, and his Gentile brothers? Because "he was afraid of criticism." To eat with someone meant that you accepted them. When the "friends of James" arrived, it was like a middle school lunch scene. In middle school, you might have sat with the kids who were not cool, but then when the cool kids walked by, you got up because you wanted to be included with the cool kids. That's what Peter was doing in Antioch. But at God's table of grace, *all* his kids are the cool kids. Jesus welcomes *all* to the banquet table of Abraham.[9] At the table of grace, there is no "separate but equal."

Peter had experienced the power of the gospel when he went into Cornelius's home, as we saw in the last chapter. Peter knew that Jews and Gentiles were equal in the family of Abraham through Jesus: he saw Gentiles receive the same Holy Spirit as Jews. Despite knowing correct doctrine, he gave in to fear. His right doctrine did not lead to right living (holiness). He feared the good ol' boys from Jerusalem more than he feared his good God. Peter's ethnocentrism caused the other believers—including Barnabas, who had brought Paul to the multiethnic church in Antioch—to be led astray.

Fear is contagious. So is courage. Choose courage.

Paul confronted Peter, Barnabas, and the others because "they were not following the truth of the gospel message" (Galatians 2:14, NLT). Ethnocentrism, racism, and indifference to racial injustice do not reflect the truth of the gospel. In the face of criticism, peer pressure, political pressure, economic pressure, and family pressure, we must love Jesus and our siblings in Christ more than we fear rejection.

Paul gave Peter the gospel by reminding him that Jews and Gentiles are made right by faith in Jesus *alone*, not by striving to fulfill the law through human effort or by the ethnic badges that make a person Jewish.

Paul was able to stand up to Peter because of the gospel. The former Jewish nationalist could no longer be a racist because Jesus had made him a gracist. When Paul said yes to Jesus, his old sin nature was crucified with Jesus, and now the resurrected Messiah lived in him. He did not fear people, because he trusted Jesus, "who loved me and gave himself for me" (Galatians 2:20, NLT).

Paul stood firm in the gospel; so must we.

The Jerusalem Council

The multiethnic church in Antioch was exploding in growth. Gentiles and Jews were coming to faith in the risen Lord Jesus. Enemies were becoming family. As we've already learned in the previous chapter, Paul and Barnabas, who had been entrusted with this initiative, were not the first to cross the barrier from Jew to Gentile with the Good News of Jesus Christ. Philip (Acts 8) and Peter (Acts 10) had already done that. Paul and Barnabas, however, were the first to establish multiethnic churches, where Jews and Gentiles worshiped together. Despite all this, a dispute arose because so many Gentiles were coming to faith:

> Some men came down from Judea and began to teach the brothers, "Unless you are circumcised according to the custom prescribed by Moses, you cannot be saved." After Paul and Barnabas had engaged them in serious argument and debate, Paul and Barnabas and some others were appointed to go up to the apostles and elders in Jerusalem about this issue. . . .
>
> When they arrived at Jerusalem, they were welcomed by the church, the apostles, and the elders, and they reported all that God had done with them. But some of the believers who belonged to the party of the Pharisees stood up and said, "It is necessary to circumcise them [the Gentiles] and to command them to keep the law of Moses."
>
> ACTS 15:1-2, 4-5

So, what's going on? Some Messianic Jews were defending and holding on to the ethnic boundary markers of being Jewish. Remember, in the ancient world, a person's ethnicity was not about the color of their skin but about their religious practices. These Jews wanted Gentiles to become ethnic Jews by taking on circumcision.

What they needed to understand was that faith that led to circumcision of the heart (regeneration) and baptism were the external boundary markers of God's new, Jew-Gentile people through the victory of the Messiah.[10] Jews were free to keep their ethnic boundaries, and Gentiles were free to not be circumcised. Faith and baptism now distinguished God's people. Jesus alone saves—not one's ethnicity or moral performance. Paul writes,

> When you came to Christ, you were "circumcised," but not by a physical procedure. Christ performed a spiritual circumcision—the cutting away of your sinful nature. For you were buried with Christ when you were baptized. And with him you were raised to new life because you trusted the mighty power of God, who raised Christ from the dead. You were dead because of your sins and because your sinful nature was not yet cut away. Then God made you alive with Christ, for he forgave all our sins.
>
> COLOSSIANS 2:11-13, NLT

These issues came to a head among the church's leadership, and they met in Jerusalem to discuss them:

> The apostles and the elders gathered to consider this matter. After there had been much debate, Peter

stood up and said to them, "Brothers, you are aware that in the early days God made a choice among you, that by my mouth the Gentiles would hear the gospel message and believe. And God, who knows the heart, bore witness to them by giving them the Holy Spirit, just as he also did to us. He made no distinction between us and them, cleansing their hearts by faith. Now then, why are you testing God by putting a yoke on the disciples' necks that neither our ancestors nor we have been able to bear? On the contrary, we believe that we are saved through the grace of the Lord Jesus in the same way they are."

The whole assembly became silent and listened to Barnabas and Paul describe all the signs and wonders God had done through them among the Gentiles.

ACTS 15:6-12

Even today, we have issues around faith, identity, and behavior. One example of the way cultural differences still divide God's church is the Church of God denomination. A Black ordained minister of the Church of God named Willian Seymour was used by God to birth the modern-day Pentecostal movement. In my book *Building a Multiethnic Church*, I wrote that when the Azusa Street Revival began April 9, 1906, it was "national news because Blacks, Whites, Hispanics, Asians, and Native Americans all worshiped together. In a time of racism and segregation, the gospel of grace broke down the walls of segregation and racism and birthed a reconciled and unified people. As Frank Bartleman, a minister in Los Angeles who witnessed the Azusa Street Revival, said, 'The color line was washed away in the blood.'"[11]

This epic move of God started out multiethnic but quickly segregated itself into Black and White. In 1912, a group of "white leaders encouraged African American leaders to establish their own national event. The stated reason was that the large numbers of African Americans in attendance deterred whites from attending."[12] The Black pastors created the National Association of the Church of God in response to this racism.

This was sinful and a betrayal of the gospel. White supremacy, or any other form of ethnic supremacy, is a sin that was crucified in the body of Jesus. Unlike other early White Church of God leaders who "often defied segregation laws by holding interracial worship events," these pastors lacked the gospel courage to have a unified conference.[13]

The Jerusalem Council could have *easily* gone in the direction of starting Messianic Jewish congregations only, and then starting various Gentile congregations based on different ethnicities. This would have been easier. Why put up with all the headaches of getting different people together in the gospel?

But Jesus does not call us to do what is easy. He calls us to be faithful. Jesus expresses himself differently and beautifully through our colors and our cultures. There is no ethnic superiority in the Messiah because we, together, are clothed in Christ. Our ethnic diversity is an opportunity for celebrating, not erasing. Paul writes, "God has put the body [of Christ] together, giving greater honor to the less honorable, so that there would be no division in the body, but that the members would have the same concern for each other" (1 Corinthians 12:24-25).

Back to the Jerusalem Council. James, the half brother of Jesus, addressed the council:

Brothers, listen to me. [Peter] has reported how God first intervened to take from the Gentiles a people for his name. And the words of the prophets agree with this, as it is written:

After these things, I will return
and rebuild David's fallen tent.
I will rebuild its ruins
and set it up again,
so that the rest of humanity
may seek the Lord—
even all the Gentiles
who are called by my name—
declares the Lord
who makes these things known from long ago.

Therefore, in my judgment, we should not cause difficulties for those among the Gentiles who turn to God, but instead we should write to them to abstain from things polluted by idols, from sexual immorality, from eating anything that has been strangled, and from blood. For since ancient times, Moses has had those who proclaim him in every city, and every Sabbath day he is read aloud in the synagogues.

ACTS 15:13-21

James gave his Gentile siblings four prohibitions that correspond to the ones given to the Gentiles who sojourn among Jews in Leviticus 17–18. Basically, James was saying that the Gentiles could not participate in idolatry. The gospel frees us to be who we're meant to be—a beautiful family of different people, walking in holiness, joining Jesus on his mission to reconcile the world to himself by serving the world.

Love Is the Color of Worship

In AD 49, the Roman emperor Claudius kicked the Jews out of Rome because Messianic Jews were debating traditional Jews in the synagogue and "constantly made disturbance at the instigation of Chrestus."[14] While the Messianic Jews were out of Rome from AD 49 to AD 54, the Gentile followers of Jesus were growing and leading the Roman house churches. In AD 54, Emperor Nero allowed the Jews to return to Rome. When the Messianic Jews returned to their churches, they found Gentiles leading. Immediately, ethnic tensions arose because the Jews thought they were God's people and that the Gentiles were let into Abraham's family as an afterthought. In addition, the Gentiles acted with ethnic superiority and began to look down on their Jewish siblings. Paul describes this conflict:

> You Gentiles, who were branches from a wild olive tree, have been grafted in. So now you also receive the blessing God has promised Abraham and his children, sharing in the rich nourishment from the root of God's special olive tree. But you must not brag about being grafted in to replace the branches that were broken off. You are just a branch, not the root.
>
> "Well," you may say, "those branches were broken off to make room for me." Yes, but remember— those branches were broken off because they didn't believe in Christ, and you are there because you do believe. So don't think highly of yourself, but fear what could happen. For if God did not spare the original branches, he won't spare you either.
>
> ROMANS 11:17-21, NLT

Whether it be White supremacy, Black supremacy, or any kind of supremacy, God will judge it. If God's people are acting just like the world, choosing power and privilege over the Kingdom, what good are we to the world?

How did Paul convince these Jews and Gentiles to pursue the only supremacy that matters—the supremacy of Jesus?

He did it by teaching them to *worship*. When we worship Jesus and find our identity in him and what he accomplished for us, it moves us to pursue Jesus' supremacy:

> Therefore, brothers and sisters, in view of the mercies of God, I urge you to present your bodies as a living sacrifice, holy and pleasing to God; this is your true worship. Do not be conformed to this age, but be transformed by the renewing of your mind, so that you may discern what is the good, pleasing, and perfect will of God.
>
> ROMANS 12:1-2

Paul reminded the Jews and Gentiles in Rome of "the mercies of God," the redeeming work of King Jesus. As we keep our gaze on Jesus and respond to his grace, we choose to become living sacrifices. By becoming living sacrifices, "holy and pleasing to God," we love each other through our shared identity in Christ. Therefore, listening to, learning from, and loving our siblings of other ethnicities become offerings of worship to Jesus. Temples are created for worship, right? We collectively are the temple of God,[15] and *love is the color of worship*. At the Cross and through the Resurrection, the Jewish, Black, White, Asian, Latino, and Indigenous person are all saved by grace and placed in Abraham's family so we can love each other.

Paul then instructed the first Christians to "be transformed by the renewing of [their] mind[s]." Jews and Gentiles viewed each other from the world's perspective, just as we often do today. Paul was saying that Jesus will transform a person by renewing their mind to think about and to see their siblings the way he does.

Through constant exposure to, meditation on, and application of the gospel to how we see ourselves and each other in Christ, our minds are transformed to value our siblings. When we look down on another person in Christ, we are betraying the gospel by disobedience.

What is God's good, pleasing, and perfect will for his multiethnic family? The rest of Romans 12 tells us. So much of the racial divide in God's family is because of spiritual ignorance and a lack of faith to live out the gospel.

Look at the logic of Paul. First, he reminded the mixed congregations in Rome that Jesus' body has many parts but is one and that people should "not to think of [themselves] more highly than [they] should think" (Romans 12:3). The gospel is the antidote to ethnic supremacy and the pride of spiritual giftedness.[16] This is true of us today. How in the world can we think more highly of ourselves when we view the spectacular cross of Jesus? How can we look down on our siblings in Christ when we remember that we collectively are Jesus' body?

When you look at a Black Christian, you are looking at the body of Jesus.

When you look at an Asian Christian, you are looking at the body of Jesus.

When you look at a White, Latino, or Indigenous Christian, you are looking at the body of Jesus.

The way we love each other is worship. Love is the color of worship.

As we've seen, God's plan all along was to give to Abraham a multiethnic family. This plan was finally accomplished in the life, death, and resurrection of Jesus and in the outworking of Jesus' body, the church. The body of Christ is how Jesus manifests himself in the world. Love is the vision for Christ's new community, and the love of God provides the blueprint for how to heal our racial divide.

I hope you've caught the Bible's vision of what a unified church looks like. In the next section of this book, we'll look at color-blessed discipleship and how the Bible's vision might look in today's context.

| | | | **MARINATE ON THIS** | | | |

PRAYER

> Father,
> As you did with Paul, remove the scales from my eyes that I
>   may see Jesus
> and the bigness of his gospel.
>
> King Jesus,
> In the face of criticism, may I look at your face of grace
> and refuse to cower to racism.
>
> Holy Spirit,
> Remind me that I have been crucified with Christ and
>   that I no longer live,
> but that Christ the King lives in me.
> He is the one who loved me and gave himself for me.
> Therefore, like Paul, when racism rears its ugly head,
> I will confront it with the gospel of grace.
> In Jesus' name,
> Amen.

THINGS TO THINK ABOUT

- Our God does not waste anything—the good, the bad, or the ugly. He doesn't squander the people, places, and predicaments of our lives. Our Father in heaven, through the beautiful mystery of his loving providence, uses our backgrounds, culture, and life experiences as a canvas to recreate us into his ambassadors of reconciliation.

- Ethnocentrism, racism, and indifference to racial injustice are not following the truth of the gospel. In the face of criticism, peer pressure, political pressure, economic pressure, and family pressure, we must love Jesus and our siblings in Christ more than we fear rejection.

- Jesus expresses himself differently and beautifully through our colors and our cultures. There is no ethnic superiority in the Messiah because we, together, are clothed in Christ. Our ethnic diversity is an opportunity for celebrating, not erasing.

QUESTIONS TO DISCUSS

1. Paul's birth, background, and life experiences made him ideally suited to be the apostle to the Gentiles. In what ways has God uniquely equipped you to help heal our racial divide? What skills, gifts, and experiences do you have to offer? (If you're having trouble thinking of any, ask a trusted friend or mentor.)

2. The believers were first called "Christians" in Antioch because they were no longer Jewish and Gentile but something new altogether. How does our belief in Jesus unite different ethnicities together? How should the Jerusalem Council's decision—not to establish separate Jew and Gentile congregations, but united congregations of Christians—affect our churches today?

3. "Love is the color of worship." How does a focus on worshiping Jesus help overcome ethnic supremacy? How can you make worship more of a focus in your discipleship?

GOSPEL BEHAVIORS TO PRACTICE

Today, reflect on why you may be afraid to talk about God's multiethnic gospel and ask God to show you where you need to repent from your old ways and respond in God's way.

PART 2

COLOR-BLESSED DISCIPLESHIP

CHAPTER 6

A HOLE IN OUR DISCIPLESHIP

I was with a group of church planters serving on a denomination's leadership committee when I was asked to present my theological convictions as to why Transformation Church is a multiethnic, multigenerational church shaped by the mission of Jesus. I explained that our vision is rooted in Jesus' words:

> [Jesus] said to him, "Love the Lord your God with all your heart, with all your soul, and with all your mind. This is the greatest and most important command. The second is like it: Love your neighbor as yourself. All the Law and the Prophets depend on these two commands."
>
> MATTHEW 22:37-40

Jesus came near and said to them, "All authority
has been given to me in heaven and on earth. Go,
therefore, and make disciples of all nations, baptizing
them in the name of the Father and of the Son
and of the Holy Spirit, teaching them to observe
everything I have commanded you. And remember,
I am with you always, to the end of the age."

MATTHEW 28:18-20

I explained that we are a great-commandment, great-commission church. We are called to love God, self, and our neighbors through the power and presence of the Holy Spirit. The area where Transformation Church is located is full of multiethnic and multigenerational people; therefore, they are the people we want to care for and reach with the Good News. The mission of Jesus, rooted in God's covenant with Abraham, calls us to develop intentional strategies to reach our diverse community. And, as we saw in the last section, both the great commandment (whose definition of "neighbor" Jesus expanded to include the ethnic "other" and even the enemy) and the great commission (to make disciples of "all nations [*ethnos*]") are specifically related to bringing diverse people together in Christ. This is what it means to be mission shaped.

After I finished presenting, silence filled the room. One by one, the White pastors began to challenge me, not with Scripture but with stories of how Black people or people of color did not come to their churches or would come but not stay. They went on to say that it was cool that I was doing a multiethnic church but that it is not for everyone. Some people just want to be with people like themselves, and we should create environments for that to happen. I thought to myself, *I just can't imagine the apostle Paul saying, "I am going to plant a church for Greeks, and a church for Italians, and a church for Jews, and a church for Africans because people like to be with people like themselves."* When we are in bubbles of sameness, we are trapped in rooms of ignorance. It is through our differences, in the midst of the beautiful struggle of grace, that deep transformation occurs.

After the negative response from this church planting committee, I sat silently. I was mad, but I felt that if I raised my voice, I would be pegged as the angry Black man, so I just marinated and prayed. After a few moments of awkward silence, a Puerto Rican leader of the denomination gently said, "Brothers, Derwin is right. The Scriptures bear witness to what he was saying. The future of the church is to return and learn afresh from the early church. The early church was a multiethnic church."

Over the years since that meeting, many of those same pastors individually have asked me to help them learn how to lead a church that reaches and builds a multiethnic family that loves Jesus and each other. If overcoming racial division were easy, we would have accomplished it by now. It is *not* easy. That's why we need the power of God to help us reimagine what the church can be and our roles in making it so. If you follow Jesus, you are his body—his church. It's not just the pastor's or staff's job to make this happen. *You* are a royal priest and have authority in Christ to be the change you want to see.[1]

And that's what we'll explore in the next several chapters. In the first part of this book, we examined how the Holy Spirit was healing the racial divide among the first Christians in the early church as God fulfilled his promise to Abraham through the work of Jesus Christ. Now in this second part, we will discover what it might look like for this racial divide to be healed in our churches today. Complete unity will not happen until the new heaven and new earth. Until that day, we are a signpost pointing to that glorious future.

The Bar Is Too Low

In the church, we have set the bar too low for having a racist attitude. Often racists are portrayed as people who are involved in the KKK or another hate group or who have Nazi swastikas tattooed on their shoulders. We think racists are people we can easily identify by some outward allegiance or display. More importantly, we draw the line for what constitutes racism somewhere beyond our own attitudes and beliefs to make sure the label never touches our own hearts. However, racist attitudes and institutional structures can be much more subtle and just as damaging.

Racism is both individual and systemic (institutional). Individual racism or prejudice is the belief or doctrine that one's ethnic group is superior to another; thus, the domination or unequal treatment of the group you see as inferior is normalized. For example, think of how Native Americans were considered savages or people of African descent were enslaved or of apartheid in South Africa.

Systemic or institutional racism is racism codified in laws, policies, or governmental systems that favor one ethnic group over another. This can mean actively harming these other groups or working to preserve power and advantages for the favored ethnic group. One example of systemic racism is the grandfather clause, which was a "constitutional device enacted by seven Southern states between 1895 and 1910 to deny suffrage to African Americans. It provided that those who had enjoyed the right to vote prior to 1866 or 1867, and their lineal descendants, would be exempt from recently enacted educational, property, or tax requirements for voting. Because the former slaves had not been granted the franchise until the adoption of the Fifteenth Amendment in 1870, those clauses worked effectively to exclude Black people from the vote but assured the franchise to many impoverished and illiterate whites."[2] Or how the G.I. Bill "was structured in a way that ultimately shut doors for the 1.2 million Black veterans who had bravely served their country during World War II, in segregated ranks." As a result, "the wide disparity in the bill's implementation ended up helping drive growing gaps in wealth, education and civil rights between white and Black Americans."[3]

As a pastor, for years now, I have counseled and discipled people who are working through racism. The Lord has worked and is working in my own heart to rid it of prejudice. That's what the gospel does. It defeats and overcomes all forms of sin if we allow Jesus to work in us. If we drop our pride and pick up our crosses, he will transform us.

Overt racism is real. But I am very concerned about the subtle racism that Christians have allowed into their lives.

I am concerned about the racism through which a Christian does not love their neighbor of another ethnicity as they love themselves. Love is sacrificial and costly, not a platitude that rings hollow.

I am concerned about the racism that produces paternalistic actions of progressives that reveal they think they know what is best for people of color.

I am concerned about the racism that is seen only as an individual sin issue but dismisses the historic systemic racial injustice that is baked into existing structures that have governed American society.[4]

I am concerned about how "homogenous local churches reproduce inequality, encourage oppression, strengthen racial division, and heighten political separation."[5]

I am concerned about the racism of a Christian who intentionally remains silent in the face of racial injustice toward their brothers and sisters of different ethnicities and about disunity in the church and the broader culture.

I am concerned about the racism that causes a Christian parent to refuse to let their child marry a Christian of a different ethnicity simply because of the color of their skin. This mindset in essence says, "You can be my brother in Christ but not my brother-in-law." This is what ethnic supremacy looks like.

In a recent conversation with a White brother who said he was a Christian, I asked him how he felt about Black people. He said, "I do not have a problem with them." I asked him to show in Scripture where Jesus says, "Love God with your heart, mind, soul, and strength. And do not have a problem with your neighbor."

King Jesus calls us as his people to love God with the totality of our being and to love our neighbors the way we love ourselves.

If I do not love you as I love myself, I am not going to advocate on your behalf.

If I do not love you as I love myself, I am not going to be concerned about your pain.

If I do not love you as I love myself, I am not going to seek justice when the noose of injustice is suffocating you.

I have had similar conversations with Black and Latino brothers in Christ, who have equally prejudiced attitudes toward other ethnicities. Prejudice is not a one-way street. It is a traffic jam that can only be cleared by Christ-generated, Holy Spirit–empowered love that is "humble" and thinks of "others as better than yourselves." The apostle Paul tells us, "Don't look out only for your own interests, but take an interest in others, too" (Philippians 2:3-4, NLT).

Racism and prejudice are cancers that affect all ethnic groups. Learning to love each other—to *really* love each other as God has commanded and as God has empowered us—takes an act of courageous faith to tell the truth, to offer grace, to extend kindness, and to be the change you want to see in the world.

When you love someone, you sacrifice on their behalf.

When you love someone, their pain is your pain.

When you love someone, the injustice they experience matters to you.

When you love someone, there is no "us versus them." There is only "us" in Christ.

When you love someone, you love them the way you love yourself.

Those who love their brothers and sisters in Christ of a different ethnicity the way they love themselves are on their way to healing the racial divide. Love heals the hurt. Love undoes injustice. Love is the bridge that connects the disconnected. Love takes a sledgehammer of grace and breaks down the barriers that divide us: "For Christ himself has brought peace to us. He united Jews and Gentiles into one people when, in his own body on the cross, he broke down the wall of hostility that separated us" (Ephesians 2:14, NLT).

Are you willing to be Jesus' sledgehammer of grace?

Colorblind vs. Color Blessed

Colorblind ideology is prevalent in the American church. Often those who say "I don't see color" are thought to be virtuous. I get the sentiment behind the statement, but it is flawed and damaging. It is flawed because God created our different ethnicities and colors.[6] Every human being is an image-bearer of God, and their unique ethnicity is a mirror that reflects God's image back into the world. To not see the beauty in our diverse colors and cultures is to not see an aspect of God's creative genius. I have found when White brothers and sisters say they do not see color, it is because their color has not been a historic disadvantage to them and their ancestors. Colorblind ideology also creates a false sense that everything is okay. It acts like a spiritual sleeping aid that causes us to ignore certain injustices.

Colorblindness is an illusion. Racism and prejudice are everywhere, and while they may at times be hidden, they have a tendency to reveal themselves in high-pressure situations and conflict. For example, in the championship game of the 2020 Euro Cup between England and Italy, three Black players from England's team—Marcus Rashford, Jadon Sancho, and Bukayo Saka—missed crucial penalty kicks that could have given England a massive victory. Afterward, the Black players were the targets of racist abuse, including when "a mural in the city of Manchester, England, depicting Rashford, celebrating his charitable work, was defaced in a way police have called 'racially aggravated.'" The racist abuse these three Black players received was so bad that the British prime minister tweeted, "This England team deserve to be lauded as heroes, not racially abused on social media. Those responsible for this appalling abuse should be ashamed of themselves."[7]

Sadly, historically and today, discrimination is reality in

the church and outside the church. Have things gotten better than they've been in the past? Sure. But there is so much more in Christ and his gospel that we need to claim.

Colorblind ideology is bad theology. It diminishes the glory of God. It is damaging because people of color feel unseen and unvalued. In all my years on earth, and in twenty-plus years of ministry, I have never heard a White person say to another White person, "I do not see your color. I am colorblind."

While I was sipping on a bold, black cup of coffee and working on this book in a coffee shop, an older White gentleman noticed me and asked me what I was doing. When I told him I was writing a book on how to heal the racial divide, he told me that there was no racial divide in America and that he did not see color. I said, "Brother, why not? God made me this way, and he made you the way you are. He wants you to appreciate my beautiful color, just as he wants me to appreciate your beautiful color." In recognizing our different "colors," we are acknowledging our equality in Christ as children of Abraham. In the new heaven and new earth, we take our colors and ethnicities with us.[8]

Just as colorblind ideology has distracted the church from its mission of reconciliation, color-blessed discipleship will help us fulfill our mission of reconciliation.[9] God, in an act of unmatched grace, reconciled us to himself so we could experience the joy of siblingship. Our God is a God of reconciliation.

Color-blessed discipleship is the process by which God the Holy Spirit forms Christ in the family he promised to Abraham.[10] In the Spirit's power, as we yield to his loving initiatives, God's kids learn to love, value, advocate for, and celebrate each other's ethnic and cultural differences. We learn to lay our lives down for one another.[11]

Color-blessed disciples understand that ethnic reconciliation is intrinsic to the gospel of Jesus Christ. Gone are the days of believing Jesus accomplished reconciliation only vertically. The reconciliation of Jesus is vertical *and* horizontal. You cannot have one without the other. It's not a fad or a trend; rather, as we have already seen, it is at the center of the gospel.[12]

Color-blessed discipleship understands that God in Christ gives us the Good News so we can be good family members, blessing one another and pursuing justice on behalf of one another. Our love for one another proves that we are Jesus' disciples.[13]

As we continue through this book, I am going to guide you through several practices that will help you cultivate a life of color-blessed discipleship. It will take a discipleship revolution to heal the racial divide because currently there is a hole in our discipleship.

A Hole in Our Discipleship

The American church has a hole in its discipleship. Minister and activist John M. Perkins writes,

The problem is that there is a gaping hole in our
gospel. We have preached a gospel that leaves
us believing that we can be reconciled to God
but not reconciled to our Christian brothers
and sisters who don't look like us—brothers and
sisters with whom we are, in fact, one blood.[14]

It is past time to fill this hole. Our gospel is too individualistic and consumeristic. Dr. Soong-Chan Rah writes,

The American church, in taking its cues from
Western, white culture, has placed at the center
of its theology and ecclesiology the primacy of the
individual. The cultural captivity of the church
has meant that the church is more likely to reflect
the individualism of Western philosophy than
the value of community found in Scripture. The
individualistic philosophy that has shaped Western
society, and consequently shaped the American
church, reduces Christian faith to a personal,
private and individual faith.[15]

Our American gospel leaves little to no room for ethnic reconciliation, because the gospel has been turned into a
story of self-fulfillment instead of Christ's fulfillment of God's
promise to Abraham. We think Jesus saves us just for *us*. But
the redeeming achievement of Jesus creates a family, and his
grace is given to us so that, by the Spirit, we can be healthy,

loving, mature members of this family that God promised Abraham. Jesus was faithful to do his part. Now we must be faithful to do our part to grow and mature. This Spirit-driven process is called *progressive sanctification.* Through it, we give Jesus more and more access to transform us into living sacrifices. Living sacrifices love, listen to, learn from, repent with, and serve their brothers and sisters in Christ.[16]

Historically, one of the reasons racism has been able to find a host in the American church is because we have viewed the work of Jesus individualistically. For example, if Jesus' primary job is to save our souls, then justice in the present on earth doesn't really matter. In this reductionist view, the marginalized and the oppressed will be free in heaven, so what happens on earth—other than salvation—is less important. This narrow view of salvation is one of the reasons the evangelical church largely did not participate in the Civil Rights Movement of the 1960s and still struggles with justice issues today. Historian Matthew J. Hall writes,

In all of my research on the long history of racial justice and the black freedom movement, I find that my fellow churchmen who supported the cause of justice were more often the exception, not the rule. Instead, my research—and that of historians far more accomplished than me—makes quite clear that white evangelicals throughout the South were overwhelmingly opposed to the civil rights movement. . . . Those who denounced the civil rights movement routinely trotted out the allegation that the cause was fundamentally about "mixing the races" and marrying off blacks and whites. For many southern whites, the thought of their white daughter married and sexually united to a black man was unfathomable.[17]

Historian Carolyn Renée Dupont adds,

Simply put, any suggestion that the religion of southern whites aided the civil rights struggle grossly perverts the past. While many evangelicals displayed kindness in their personal dealings with blacks, most also enthusiastically defended a system designed to advantage whites and to correspondingly disadvantage African Americans at every turn. . . . Evangelicals resisted black equality in many ways. Some ministers preached an overt biblical sanction for segregation. Most preachers took a more oblique approach, remaining silent about black equality while condemning faith-based civil rights activism as "a prostitution of the church for political purposes." Most southern Christians did not regard segregation as a sin, and they resented those who criticized their "way of life."[18]

An individualized faith means that a person's faith in Jesus is a personal, private matter. This view creates a "me" mentality and does not challenge prejudices and racial indifference.

Color-blessed disciples understand that the gospel moves us from "What about *me*?" to "What about *we*?" We are the diverse family of God. Our siblingship and place in the body of Christ take precedence over everything. Our allegiance is to King Jesus and each other.

Regardless of your birth ethnicity, when you go through the waters of baptism, you are identifying with Jesus' death and resurrection. This external display of the internal, eternal reality of being united to him means that you are also united to believers in the underground church in China and the ancient church in Iran, to the Pentecostals in Brazil, to the Anglicans in Nigeria, and to believers all over the world. Color-blessed disciples see themselves as participating in a global family. We become a community of siblings, preserving the unity that Jesus won through his sacrificial death and resurrection. Together, Black, White, Yellow, Brown—we are the blood-bought mosaic that forms the body of Christ. To not love or advocate on behalf of, seek justice for, and serve your siblings in Christ of a different ethnicity is to not love Jesus.

Racism and prejudice, like cancerous tumors, hide within the body of Christ because many pastors know if they confront racism, they will pay a price. Here, for example, is an email I received:

Pastor Derwin,

Thank you so much for what you and Transformation Church are doing. Our pastor recently preached a sermon on racism. He got so many negative emails from our White congregation threatening to leave that the following Sunday, he apologized for making them feel uncomfortable. My wife and I decided to leave. We are White with two adopted Black sons. I could no longer look them in the eyes and see them being spiritually hurt in this toxic environment. Please pray for us.

Recently I tweeted, "Over the last year, many of my White pastor siblings are discouraged and heartbroken over people leaving their church because they are preaching more on how the gospel overcomes the sins of racism and systemic injustice."[19] I invited my Twitter followers to share their stories, and I received over fifty replies. One reply (sent privately through Twitter and lightly edited to preserve privacy) particularly broke my heart:

Over one thousand people have left our church since I called out [the White supremacy rally in] Charlottesville and reminded our people "only Jesus is supreme." And by the way, I'm bold and stubborn but very loving, gentle, and measured with my words. Yet we "beat people up over race," "White people are second-class citizens," and "it's all Pastor talks about." Never mind one would be hard-pressed to find a staff more committed to the exaltation of Jesus and His Word. Sigh. And then George Floyd and the Chauvin trial. . . . Still more loss, anger, and cost. It is idolatry and sinister and sick.

Color-blessed disciples refuse to bow down and appease the sin of racism in fear of retribution. Pray for your pastor to be courageous.

Racism has been able to suck the life out of the body of Christ because many resist the sanctifying, transforming work of the Spirit. The Bible calls this transformation "holiness." Holiness means that because of "the mercies of God," we become "a living sacrifice" (Romans 12:1). We begin to sin less by relying on the Spirit more, including giving Jesus our racist thoughts and stereotypes.

This is a work that needs to happen in all of us. On a flight after 9/11, I saw a group of men that I perceived to be Muslim because of how they looked. As my mind was filling with ignorant, fearful, dehumanizing thoughts, I sensed the Holy Spirit saying, *Derwin, how do you feel when you are racially profiled? How do you feel when people judge you before they get to know you?*

I repented. I was wrong. Immediately, I prayed and asked for the Lord's forgiveness. I didn't even realize I held those beliefs until fear pushed it out of me. Over the years, I have shared this experience with my Transformation Church congregation and at conferences. None of us are exempt from prejudice because none of us are wholly sanctified yet. I must renew my mind daily and seek the Spirit's power to love people as I have been loved by Jesus. Loving people is so much better than fearing people.

We need to be honest about our racial prejudices and stereotypes. The Lord will heal what we reveal. Not only do

I pastor people from the Middle East or of Middle Eastern descent, but now one of my best friends is from Pakistan. He is a former Muslim who met Jesus through a dream, and he became a pastor in Charlotte, North Carolina. I love him. He is my brother. The same blood that runs through Jesus' veins runs through ours. We are not united by the color of our skin; we are united by the color of Jesus' blood.

Things Have Gotten Harder

After the murder of George Floyd by a police officer in May 2020, I saw an awakening of White brothers and sisters in Christ to what had been going on for a long time. It was like the COVID-19 pandemic slowed everything down enough so that this horrific moment could not be overlooked. I saw openness unlike any time before, especially in the church. But I have also seen a hardening from many Christians. I have had so many conversations where some of my White brothers and sisters fight harder to prove that racism is not a real issue than they do actually fighting racism through the gospel. They will say things like "White supremacy is not a problem; it's just a few people." But even the government acknowledges the increasing scope of the issue. FBI Director Christopher A. Wray testified in 2021,

> When it comes to racially-motivated violent extremism, that number—again, number of investigations and number of arrests—has grown

significantly on my watch. . . . And the number of arrests, for example, of racially motivated violent extremists who are what you would categorize as white supremacists, last year was almost triple the number it was in my first year as director.[20]

From the 2016 presidential election until the present, I have experienced an increase in the number of negative emails and divisive interactions I've received for preaching that the gospel heals, forgives, seeks racial justice, and unites people of different ethnicities. Those who disagree with me sound like the talking points of their favorite cable news anchors that support their brand of political ideology. Often the same people who were angry with NFL players for taking a knee during the national anthem to peacefully protest police brutality and racial injustice were strangely silent when an angry White mob beat a police officer with an American flag at the US Capitol insurrection.

As I write this chapter, hate crimes against Asian people in America, many of which are perpetrated by Black people, have increased dramatically since the COVID-19 global pandemic began.[21] I have heard political leaders say racist things, like calling COVID-19 "kung flu" or the "China virus" when talking about it. When political leaders use racist rhetoric, it emboldens people prone to racial violence to act on their feelings of hate. When words are used to dehumanize people, it becomes easier to treat people inhumanely.

Racism, racial disunity, and racial injustice are cancer in

the body of Christ and in our world. The idea that we can know Jesus and not love our brothers and sisters in Christ of a different ethnic background is an abomination. The apostle John writes,

> We love because [God] first loved us. If anyone says, "I love God," and yet hates his brother or sister, he is a liar. For the person who does not love his brother or sister whom he has seen cannot love God whom he has not seen. And we have this command from him: The one who loves God must also love his brother and sister.
>
> I JOHN 4:19-21

Healing the racial divide is going to require people to be unwavering in their allegiance to Jesus and his gospel. For such a time as this, you are being raised up to be this person.

What follows, then, is an exploration of five marks of color-blessed discipleship. In these chapters, we will learn that color-blessed disciples trust the supremacy of Christ, engage in difficult conversations, collectively mourn injustice, display gospel character, and affirm the Reconciler's Creed. As we've already seen, the church was birthed in a time of ethnic division and racism. By God's grace, in Jesus, and with the Holy Spirit's help, I believe the church can heal our racial divide today.

| | | | **MARINATE ON THIS** | | | |

PRAYER

> *Father,*
> *By grace through faith in your beloved Son,*
> *I am now a member of the beautifully diverse family*
> *   that you promised Abraham.*
> *In your family, there is no favoritism.*
> *We are equal in your sight, and we are your delight.*
>
> *Lord Jesus,*
> *Teach me to love like you do.*
> *Teach me to see every person as an image-bearer of God,*
> *   worthy of love, respect, and dignity.*
>
> *Holy Spirit,*
> *Give me the courage to cast aside prejudice and*
> *   racial biases.*
> *Give me the strength to confront evil in the world*
> *   and evil in myself.*
> *Give me power in this hour to heal our racial*
> *   divide.*
> *In Jesus' name,*
> *Amen.*

THINGS TO THINK ABOUT

- If overcoming racial division were easy, we would have accomplished it by now. It is *not* easy. That's why we need the power of God to help us reimagine what the church can be and our roles in making it so.

- Racism and prejudice are cancers that affect all ethnic groups. Learning to love each other—to *really* love each other as God has commanded and as God has empowered us to do—takes an act of courageous faith to tell the truth, to offer grace, to extend kindness, and to be the change we want to see in the world.

- Color-blessed disciples understand that the gospel moves us from "What about *me?*" to "What about *we?*" We are the diverse family of God. Our siblingship and place in the body of Christ take precedence over everything. Our allegiance is to King Jesus and each other.

QUESTIONS TO DISCUSS

1. "In the church, we have set the bar too low for having a racist attitude" (page 126). How do you react to the statement that racism is not always individual and overt but also institutional and subtle? Why do you think you reacted this way?

2. What is the distinction between "colorblind" and "color-blessed"? What examples of colorblind ideology have you seen in the church? How might those examples be different with a color-blessed perspective?

3. How does an individualist perspective hinder the necessary work to heal our racial divide? How might viewing the gospel collectively fill the "hole in our discipleship"?

GOSPEL BEHAVIORS TO PRACTICE

Practice thinking collectively about discipleship. Consider what spiritual practices you do on your own on a daily basis (Scripture reading, prayer, singing worship songs, etc.). How can you invite someone else—particularly of another ethnicity—into these practices this week?

CHAPTER 7

TRUST THE SUPREMACY OF CHRIST

It was a normal day. I was going about my business. I had just wrapped up sermon prep at my favorite coffeehouse, and I was in my Jeep at a busy intersection. I had the windows rolled down, enjoying the sixty-five-degree, sunny North Carolina day, when a big truck with three White guys drove past. As they sped past me, I heard them yell, "N—!"

Typically, I would have prayed for these young men, asking Jesus to heal their hateful hearts. But this time, something in me snapped. I'm not sure if it was hated-filled emails calling me a race baiter that had gotten the best of me or if it was watching neo-Nazis march through Charlottesville, Virginia. Maybe it was thinking about the Mother Emanuel shooting in which a White supremacist killed nine Black people after they had invited him into their Bible study. Whatever it was, before I knew it, I floored it. I found myself darting through traffic like a NASCAR driver chasing these guys. After about two miles, I pulled up beside them at a stoplight. I yelled, "What did you say?"

One of them said with a tremble in his voice, "We didn't say anything." Terror filled their eyes. They looked to be in their early twenties.

When I saw their faces, my anger dissipated. They drove off when the light turned green, and I pulled over to talk with Jesus. I repented for allowing them to draw me into the circle of hate. No one can make me act like I don't follow Jesus unless I give them power to do so. In that moment, I gave a word with an ugly history—a word that does not define me or Black people—the power to take my love away. There was no righteous anger in me. It was just anger. I wanted to do violence to them. But that would have made me no better than them.

I repented for scaring these young men. Yes, they called me the N-word. Yes, they sinned against me. But I did not have to return sin for sin. In the power of the risen Messiah, I do not have to seek retribution. The cycle of violence must be broken by people of love. Loving those young men who called me the N-word may not make them love me, but it keeps me from hating them. We must never allow our souls to disintegrate into hate.

I repented for driving angrily and dangerously down a

busy street. I could have caused a major accident. What if I had caught them and physically hurt them? The devil would have had a dance party at my destruction.

As I gathered myself, surrendering my hurt and my pride to Jesus, I was revived in my passion to live as a reconciler, a bridge builder, a man of peace. I was invigorated to serve and equip Transformation Church to flourish more in being a multiethnic, gospel-centered church. My resolve to help create a movement of Jesus-focused, gospel-shaped, multiethnic churches was strengthened. The future world belongs to the peacemakers. As Jesus said, "Blessed are the peacemakers, for they will be called sons of God" (Matthew 5:9).

Initially, I was anything but a peacemaker. I wanted to rip those guys to pieces. My response made me appreciate the deep discipleship of the young Black men and women of the Civil Rights era. They staged restaurant sit-ins and other nonviolent protests in the face of lynching, police beatings, and racial injustice. I could not imagine being called the N-word *and* having police dogs ripping flesh from my bones the way many of them experienced. And many, like Dr. King, paid the ultimate price with their lives.

Former Birmingham mayor William Bell describes the Civil Rights era by saying, "During that period of time you had people who were being murdered, homes being bombed, churches being bombed and there was a sense that evil would prevail."[1]

Yet in the face of this, these men and women nonviolently

but resolutely pursued justice. How? Dennis Edwards, a New Testament professor, provides an answer:

> Sections of the Bible, such as the Sermon on the Mount (Matt 5–7), encouraged African Americans and their allies to stand up to white supremacist mobs, brutal law enforcement agents, dogs, and hoses. Rather than being a sign of passivity and weakness, "turning the other cheek" (Matt 5:39) became an indictment upon such bullies as Bull Connor of Birmingham, AL, and the law enforcement agents in Selma, AL, who bloodied demonstrators marching across the Edmund Pettis Bridge on March 7, 1965.[2]

The Bible stoked the courage and fortitude of civil rights activists in the face of such atrocities.

The men and women of the Civil Rights era were able to stand in the midst of violent racism because they trusted that the only supremacy that is truly supreme is the supremacy of Jesus Christ. Jesus holds the power, and Jesus would be their vindication. As we seek to heal our racial divide today, we must do the same.

Jesus Is Supreme

Ethnic supremacy is the demonic view that a person's ethnic group is superior to another, that their own cultural expression is normative, and that their ethnic group should be the center of privilege and power. Supremacists believe they should be the ones in charge. Unfortunately, ethnic supremacy—in both overt and more subtle forms—is prevalent today, as we will see.

Any form of ethnic supremacy is sin and the offspring of demonic forces. It is the interethnic, diverse family of God who have been given the sacred task to "welcome one another, just as Christ also welcomed you, to the glory of God" (Romans 15:7). Dr. Korie Edwards, associate professor of sociology at Ohio State University, helps us to see this with her examination of the rise of multiethnic churches:

> Multiracial churches have a unique opportunity to confront white supremacy and work out the Good News in intimate community—not merely in theory or in principle, as an ethnically homogenous congregation might. . . . Multiracial churches are to be places where every person's belovedness is embraced and celebrated; where every person is able to come to the table with their gifts and skills as leaders and contributors to advance the Good News of Christ; and where no form of supremacy other than the supremacy of Christ reigns.[3]

Before Edwards, Dr. King reminded us of this gospel truth while speaking at Western Michigan University in 1963:

[W]e must never substitute a doctrine of black supremacy for white supremacy. For the doctrine of black supremacy is as dangerous as white supremacy. God is not interested merely in the freedom of black men and brown men and yellow men but God is interested in the freedom of the whole human race, the creation of a society where all men will live together as brothers.[4]

The only supremacy Jesus' people should want and promote is Jesus' supremacy of love. Look at how the apostle Paul describes the supremacy of Jesus:

Christ is the *visible image* of the invisible God.
>   He existed *before anything* was created and is *supreme over all creation*,
for through him God created *everything*
>   in the heavenly realms and on earth.
He made the things we can see
>   and the things we can't see—
such as thrones, kingdoms, rulers, and authorities in the unseen world.
>   *Everything* was created *through him* and *for him*.
He existed *before anything else*,
>   and he holds *all creation* together.
Christ is also the *head of the church*,
>   which is his body.
He is the *beginning*,

supreme over all who rise from the dead.
So he is *first in everything*.
For God in *all his fullness*
was pleased to live in Christ,
and through him God reconciled
everything to himself.
He made peace with *everything* in heaven and on earth
by means of Christ's blood on the cross.
COLOSSIANS 1:15-20, NLT, EMPHASIS ADDED

Jesus is supreme over everything, including the church. God, through Christ, "reconciled everything to himself." If we call Jesus "Lord," then he calls us to join him in rooting out the sin of racism.

The eternal Son of God became one of us to show us how to love each other in a racially divided world. Through his shed blood on the cross, our sins are eternally forgiven, and through his resurrection, we belong to a new multiethnic family. We are the family God promised to Abraham. We are born into conflict, and we are born again to heal the conflict.

Because Jesus is supreme, we are free to pursue justice with courage and love, living out of the unity that Jesus has won for us as brothers and sisters.

Justice Looks like Jesus

To follow Jesus is to be formed by Scripture. After his resurrection, Jesus joined two of the disciples on the road to

Emmaus. They were crushed because their Messiah was dead—or so they thought. The crucified and resurrected Messiah was walking with them. But before he revealed himself, he gave them a lesson:

> Jesus said to them, "You foolish people! You find
> it so hard to believe all that the prophets wrote
> in the Scriptures. Wasn't it clearly predicted that
> the Messiah would have to suffer all these things
> before entering his glory?" Then Jesus took them
> through the writings of Moses and all the prophets,
> explaining from all the Scriptures the things
> concerning himself.
>
> LUKE 24:25-27, NLT

All of Scripture testifies about Jesus. Jesus told the Pharisees that he is the key that unlocks the meaning of Scripture: "You search the Scriptures because you think they give you eternal life. But the Scriptures point to me! Yet you refuse to come to me to receive this life" (John 5:39-40, NLT). So Jesus is at the center of Scripture—he's the key to interpreting it correctly.

As we saw in part 1, the Bible, from Genesis to Revelation, is a story shaped by divine love and God's pursuit of a multiethnic people. The God of Abraham, Isaac, and Jacob—the one known as the great "I Am"—is a pursuer of people. Jesus is the magnet that draws the lost so they can be found and transformed by the Spirit.

We must not reduce eternal life to some ethereal afterlife

of floating as disembodied spirits. We are reborn from above to live above the petty divisions that have sabotaged the church for too long. In Christ, we become participants in the resurrection life for all eternity. The colorful montage of God's family shares in Jesus' eternal life and body.[5]

The apostle Paul tells us, "All Scripture is inspired by God and is profitable for teaching, for rebuking, for correcting, for *training in righteousness*, so that the man of God may be complete, equipped for every good work" (2 Timothy 3:16-17, emphasis added). The word *righteousness*, or *dikaiosūnē*, means "justice." Justice is righting wrongs and caring for the oppressed, the marginalized, the widow, the orphan, and the outcast. Justice is loving your neighbor as you love yourself. Justice looks like Jesus rebuking Pharisees and restoring the woman caught in adultery. Justice looks like Jesus overturning the money tables in the Temple and breaking down the sinful barriers of ethnocentrism and sexism when he asked the Samaritan woman for a drink. Justice looks like Jesus feeding hungry Jews on one side of the Sea of Galilee and feeding hungry Gentiles on the other. Justice looks like Jesus forgiving, healing, loving, rebuking, and teaching. Justice looks like *Jesus*. And Jesus lives in you to supply you with the power to live like him.[6]

In 1974, the great evangelical leader John Stott wrote concerning biblical justice, "We affirm that God is both the Creator and the Judge of all men. We therefore should share his concern for justice and reconciliation throughout human society and for the liberation of men and women from every kind of oppression."[7] If John Stott were alive today, he might be called "woke" for making a statement like this. If John Stott was "woke," I gladly link arms with this great man of God.

Scripture testifies that Jesus was sent on a mission to reconcile people to God the Father and to one another. We treasure *Jesus* by treasuring *one another*. Notice I say "treasuring," not just "being kind." Ethnic supremacy is thinking of yourself as better than another based on their ethnicity. It looks like ignoring, dismissing, or not advocating for others when they are being treated unfairly, among other things. It is an injustice to not leverage your life to rectify the injustice perpetrated against your brothers and sisters in Christ.

Color-blessed discipleship transforms our minds with the Good News by drawing us away from anything else we view as supreme and by pointing us toward the supremacy of Christ—we live our lives in *him*. God wants a unified family of oneness.[8] He sent his Son to endure great agony in order to fulfill his purpose, "to use the church to display his wisdom in its rich variety to all the unseen rulers and authorities in the heavenly places. This was his eternal plan" (Ephesians 3:10-11, NLT). As we pursue Jesus, we pursue justice and reconciliation, and we join God in his eternal desire to have a family. Jesus reveals the face and grace of God. He is the seed of Abraham, the promise keeper and covenant keeper. As Paul writes,

All of God's promises have been fulfilled in Christ with a resounding "Yes!" And through Christ, our

"Amen" (which means "Yes") ascends to God for
his glory. It is God who enables us, along with you,
to stand firm for Christ. He has commissioned us,
and he has identified us as his own by placing the
Holy Spirit in our hearts as the first installment
that guarantees everything he has promised us.

2 CORINTHIANS 1:20-22, NLT

God has kept his promise. Will we have the gospel courage to keep our promise to his people?

Gospel Courage

Courage is often discovered during times of discouragement.
Discouragement can break you, or the Spirit of God can use
it to make you. For my wife and me, the discouragement
we faced in planting a multiethnic church pushed us deeper
into Jesus, deeper into Scripture, deeper into the gospel,
deeper into the Kingdom of God, deeper into studying the
interethnic, diverse nature of the first Christians. The first
Christians took their cues from Jesus. They followed his
example, living out the Kingdom of God, in the power of
God, as a family of Jews and Gentiles. Jew-Gentile unity was
revolutionary. They were the new people of God—a unified,
forgiven, redeemed, reconciled family. They were the family
God had promised Abraham long ago. And so are we.

When others told us that starting a multiethnic church
would never work, Vicki and I were not going to be deterred.

Both of us are high-level, competitive athletes. Do not tell us what we can and can't do! But knowing that this is God's heart for his people, the discouragement brought us to our knees in prayer. And that is where we discovered the power to accomplish God's will.

As we dove into the living waters of Scripture, we saw the power of Jesus in action. He forgave sins, and he made enemies friends. At the heart of the Good News is God the Father's heart for reconciliation. He wants to reconcile humanity to himself vertically and humanity to each other horizontally. Vertical reconciliation with God and horizontal reconciliation with each other make a cross.

A cross-shaped life is a life of love. Love pursues racial reconciliation. Love protects the unity Jesus created by spilling his blood. When Jesus, the second person of the triune God, put on flesh and walked among us, he showed us what we were meant to be. In Jesus of Nazareth, we witness the glory of the living God on full display in a human being. The first Adam broke us. The last Adam heals us.[9]

As Jesus lived among us, he showed us how to love each other. It takes divine love and power to destroy what divides us. Jesus saw the destructive nature of racism, but he also saw that in becoming one of us, he would experience its destructive nature and defeat it.[10] We serve a God who is near—Immanuel, "God with us." He touched our pain, and he lived in our sin-sick world. He can relate to us at the deepest level.[11]

Growing up in Galilee, Jesus knew the distrust and suspicion that his Jewish kindred had for Gentiles and the same feelings that Gentiles had for Jews.[12] There was bad blood. Barriers were erected at every turn. If we really want to heal the racial divide in the church and in our culture, we must take seriously that only the blood of Jesus can give us a transfusion, making us the family God promised Abraham.

Adopted

The blood of Jesus is how God the Father adopts Jewish, Asian, Latino, White, and Black people into his family. God takes pleasure in bringing us home, caring for us, healing us, and teaching us. The apostle Paul writes,

> God decided in advance to adopt us into his own family by bringing us to himself through Jesus Christ. This is what he wanted to do, and it gave him great pleasure. So we praise God for the glorious grace he has poured out on us who belong to his dear Son. He is so rich in kindness and grace that he purchased our freedom with the blood of his Son and forgave our sins.
>
> EPHESIANS 1:5-7, NLT

God in Christ does not forgive us so we can remain prejudiced or indifferent toward the plague of racism that makes our land sick. Forgiveness of sins is the gateway to becoming a family. As family, we "share each other's burdens, and in this way obey the law of Christ" (Galatians 6:2, NLT). Forgiveness of sins is the door we walk through to receive "this wonderful message of reconciliation" (2 Corinthians 5:19, NLT). God reconciles us to himself through the blood of Jesus so we can be reconciled to each other through that same precious blood. In Christ, we have the same blood, the same Father.[13] In God's family, there is no favorite color or culture. Our adoption is solely dependent on the sinless life of Jesus, his atoning death on the cross, and his resurrection.

If God does not show favoritism, we should not either.

Jesus is our qualifier and equalizer. Because *he* is supreme, all our worth is discovered in him, not in our ethnicity, our culture, our socioeconomic status, or in being male or female. Our identity is rooted in the soil of his life-giving, unifying, sin-forgiving, reconciling blood. To be racist, prejudiced, or indifferent toward the sin of racism is to be these things toward Jesus himself, because he dwells in all of us.[14]

The old life is ruled by our corrupted sin nature and demonic forces that influence humanity toward the sins of racism, classism, and sexism. The blood of Jesus tore down these barriers. It is time for God's family to become faith-filled enough to trust the Spirit of God to live out the victory that King Jesus has won.

We have devoured each other for too long. Racism, or indifference to the problem of racism, will thrive among God's people if we continue to identify ourselves as anything other than blood-bought, reconciled, adopted siblings in Messiah Jesus. In and through the power of God the Spirit, we must learn to love our brothers and sisters in Christ more than political affiliations, more than cultural privilege and power, more than anything. The same blood that flowed from Jesus' body on the cross runs through his body on earth.

In Christ, our ethnic and cultural differences are not disintegrated, but they are integrated into each other's lives. Your cultural and ethnic differences make me better, and my cultural and ethnic differences make you better. Diversity is God's university of growth. Just as an orchestra has an array of musical instruments that create beautiful music when played in harmony, so does God's multiethnic family. Our ethnic and cultural differences are instruments of grace that play the sound of love for the world to hear. If we do not teach the world how to love, what hope is there? None.

Opening Our Eyes

Among those without the hope of the Messiah and his reconciling love, I expect racism. But in the family of Jesus, his body on earth, our unity and love for one another should—and must—be our life. There should be no ethnic division in the body.

However, due to the desires latent in us that are opposed to God (the flesh) and the demonic forces of evil, we may not realize that we are tainted by ethnic supremacy. Our eyes may be closed to our own role in maintaining a caste system or ethnic superiority over others. So part of what it means to trust in the supremacy of Christ is opening our eyes to the ways we may subtly be engaging in or enabling rival supremacies to Christ's, which is idolatry.

To illustrate how we can be blind to a system that we live in, let me share this: Do you remember writing at your desk in elementary school—the little chair with the small desktop attached to one side?[15] Most desks were made for right-handed people. Since I am right-handed, I had no problem with these desks. But my left-handed friends hated them because they weren't made for them. Writing on desks made for right-handed people is awkward and hard for left-handed people. The right-handed had "right privilege" because the desks were made for them. For us right-handed people, we never really thought about how hard it was for left-handed people to work on desks not made for them. My right-handed privilege blinded me to the struggles of left-handed people.

This may seem like a frivolous example, but in America, systemic racial injustice functions similarly. As you look at the history of America, policies that have historically governed society construct "concentric circles with white people of European descent in the center, the place of privilege and importance."[16] White Christians and White Americans, in general, have benefited from this reality. For example,

> Racial segregation in housing was not merely a project of southerners in the former slaveholding Confederacy. It was a nationwide project of the federal government in the twentieth century, designed and implemented by its most liberal leaders. Our system

of official segregation was not the result of a single law that consigned African Americans to designated neighborhoods. Rather, scores of racially explicit laws, regulations, and government practices combined to create a nationwide system of urban ghettos, surrounded by white suburbs.[17]

Another example of not recognizing attitudes of ethnic superiority is from my world as a pastor-theologian. When a person of color writes a theology book or contributes to theology study, their work is referred to as "Black theology" or "Latino theology." Yet theology written by White men of European descent is rarely called "Eurocentric theology." It is simply classified as theology. Ironically, the first great theologians of the church, after the apostles, were primarily North African. Athanasius of Alexandria, for example, was called the "Black Dwarf" by his enemies. Athanasius helped the church understand the biblical reality that Jesus was 100 percent God the eternal Son and 100 percent man.[18]

When I first became a Christian, I was immersed in White evangelicalism. From the beginning, I sensed a form of ethnic superiority underneath the words and actions of both laypeople and ministry leaders. All the theologians and preachers that were recommended to me, along with their books, were White men. I frequently heard criticisms of Black preachers and "their" theology. In these circles, Dr. Martin Luther King Jr. would be called unsaved for the alleged affairs he had, but not a word was said about Swiss theologian Karl Barth, who is considered the twentieth century's greatest theologian and who had a live-in mistress for years.[19] Not a word was said questioning the salvation of White pastor-theologians like Jonathan Edwards and George Whitefield, who owned slaves and endorsed slavery. It was like I was being told, "The White way of being a Christian is the right way of being a Christian." Many saw themselves and their cultural expression as the reference point for Christianity.

I remember in the early 2000s, Black Christians were getting involved in Reformed Christianity. By 2015, many of them were forced out of those White spaces because they believe the gospel addresses racism, racial injustice, and police brutality. Many were labeled heretics, social justice warriors, or critical race theorists. I was sad to see many of my friends being "canceled" at events where they had previously preached.

I was in a conversation recently with a White brother in Christ about systemic injustice. I love him deeply. We have been friends for years. We have watched our children transform from pudgy middle schoolers into adults. We have shared meals and tears together and preached at the same events. He told me, "Systemic injustice does not exist."

I responded, "Do you believe that the media has an agenda to oppress White evangelicals?" He said, "Yes, I do."

I said, "Do you believe White evangelicals are oppressed on the majority of American college campuses?" He said, "Yes, I do!"

I said, "Do you believe White evangelicals face discrimination in America?" He said, "Yes, I do!"

"Brother," I told him, "you *do* in fact believe that systemic injustice exists. But the systemic injustice you believe in oppresses White evangelicals."

"Well, I guess I do believe in systemic injustice," he admitted.

So I responded, "Are you willing to rethink that perhaps systemic injustice against Black people and other people of color exists?"

"No," he said, "systemic injustice does not exist."

And it's not just my friend. A Religion News Service story reported that "white evangelicals increasingly see men and white people as the primary victims of oppression. . . . [A] 2020 PRRI survey . . . found that more than 7 in 10 (71%) white evangelicals believe that discrimination against white Americans has become as big a problem as discrimination against Black Americans and other minorities."[20]

It's easy for us to become myopic and to see only the pain and injustice that affects us and those like us. But for those of us who are in Christ Jesus, we need to realize that his blood unites us in a way that makes even very different people family.

For my White siblings, it takes courage to see that you have been living in a world created for right-handed people and that left-handed people matter too. As followers of Jesus the Messiah, who is supreme and the Savior of all people, we must recognize that justice is embedded in the gospel message and that Jesus empowers us to carry it out.

US Representative Dean Phillips, a Democrat from Minnesota, learned firsthand this mental awakening that I am talking about. After the US Capitol was overrun by insurrectionists on January 6, 2021, he testified and apologized to his colleagues:

> "I'm not here this evening to seek sympathy or just to tell my story [but] rather to make a public apology," said Phillips. "For recognizing that we were sitting ducks in this room as the chamber was about to be breached. I screamed to my colleagues to follow me, to follow me across the aisle to the Republican side of the chamber, so that we could blend in—so that we could blend in."

> Phillips explained that he believed he and his colleagues would be safe from the rioters if they were mistaken for Republican lawmakers. However, he said that he realized that blending in was not a viable option for lawmakers of color.

> "So I'm here tonight to say to my brothers and sisters in Congress, and all around our country. I'm sorry. I'm sorry. For I had never understood, really understood, what privilege really means. It took a violent mob of insurrectionists and a lightning bolt moment in this very room. But now I know. Believe me, I really know," said Phillips.[21]

It takes courage to see that you live in a cultural context made for you and for people that look like you. This context has created disadvantages for those of different ethnicities, including your siblings in Christ. But it takes even more courage to do something about it.

When you challenge the dark powers of evil that influence humanity, and those who benefit from power structures, you will suffer. But it's worth it.

We believe, as many of those who suffered during the Civil Rights era, that Jesus is supreme, and because Jesus is supreme, we can have gospel courage as we confront racism and injustice. As the apostle Paul writes,

> If God is for us, who can ever be against us? Since he did not spare even his own Son but gave him up for us all, won't he also give us everything else? Who dares accuse us whom God has chosen for his own? No one—for God himself has given us right standing with himself. Who then will condemn us? No one—for Christ Jesus died for us and was raised to life for us, and he is sitting in the place of honor at God's right hand, pleading for us.
>
> Can anything ever separate us from Christ's love? Does it mean he no longer loves us if we have trouble or calamity, or are persecuted, or hungry, or destitute, or in danger, or threatened with death? . . . No, despite all these things, overwhelming victory is ours through Christ, who loved us.
>
> ROMANS 8:31-35, 37, NLT

| | | | MARINATE ON THIS | | | |

PRAYER

Father,
Give me the guts to confront injustice where it exists.
Give me the guts to confront prejudice within myself.
Give me the guts to fear no one in pursuit of your
    Kingdom and righteousness.

Lord Jesus,
There is power in your blood—
power to make enemies friends,
power to make foes family,
power to forgive and reconcile,
power to unify the divided.
Bleed on me again.
I desire your supremacy over all things.
Create in me a heart that loves like you love.

Holy Spirit,
Fill me with power so I can image forth the glory of God.
Fill me with your power so I can be an effective ambassador
    of reconciliation.
Amen, amen, amen.

THINGS TO THINK ABOUT

- Because Jesus is supreme, we are free to pursue justice with courage and love, living out of the unity that Jesus has won for us as brothers and sisters.

- Color-blessed discipleship transforms our minds with the Good News by drawing us away from anything else we view as supreme and by pointing us toward the supremacy of Christ.

- Jesus is our qualifier and equalizer. Because *he* is supreme, all our worth is discovered in him, not in our ethnicity, our culture, our socioeconomic status, or in being male or female. Our identity is rooted in the soil of his life-giving, unifying, sin-forgiving, reconciling blood. To be racist, prejudiced, or indifferent toward the sin of racism is to be these things toward Jesus himself, because he dwells in all of us.

QUESTIONS TO DISCUSS

1. How does accepting the supremacy of Christ help us in healing our racial divide? What does Christ's supremacy teach us about loving others?

2. What does it mean that "justice looks like Jesus"? How can we follow Jesus into his way of justice?

3. What rival supremacies in your life need to meet the true supremacy of Christ? Where might you need to open your eyes today to the injustices around you?

GOSPEL BEHAVIORS TO PRACTICE

Study Paul's great hymn about Jesus Christ in Colossians 1:15-20. Write down, verse by verse, one way that the truth in that verse speaks to healing our racial divide today.

CHAPTER 8

ENGAGE IN DIFFICULT CONVERSATIONS

As a little boy, I learned from my family that certain things were off-limits to discuss. We did not talk about the substance abuse that plagued family members or the violence, criminal activity, and other toxic behaviors we saw day after day.

When I was in middle school, I witnessed two family members having an argument. They both grabbed guns and pointed them in each other's faces. The last thing I remember was running down the street crying with my hands over my ears. I thank God no shots were fired that night. The horror of that event was never spoken of again. No one apologized to me. It was as if it did not happen. But it did, and I have carried that trauma for a long time.

I'm not being "soft." I'm tough as nails. I have been to hell and back. But no one, especially a child, should ever experience seeing loved ones so close to killing each other.

Living a lie creates tension in the soul of a family that can eventually rip it apart.

Family secrets that are unrevealed stay unhealed.

I am thankful that much of the darkness in my family of origin eventually came to light. Tough conversations were spoken. Forgiveness was asked for and granted. Repentance was acknowledged. Tears of mourning flowed. Reconciliation has occurred. Restoration continues.

Just as my family has dark secrets, America has dark family secrets too. As followers of Jesus, we are "children of light" (Ephesians 5:8), exposing the darkness so healing, repentance, reconciliation, and restoration can occur. That's why color-blessed discipleship involves not retreating from difficult conversations but engaging in them. Because that's how healing can occur.

America the Beautiful

America is my family. I love my country. I am grateful to be an American.

America has been and will continue to be a force for good in the world. But like all nations in a fallen, sin-afflicted world, she has had moments of monstrous evil. We need to acknowledge this. It is not unpatriotic to want to reveal our mistakes in order to heal them.

My great-great-great-great-grandfather Moses Davis fought in the Civil War against the Confederacy. He was in the 4th Regiment, United States Colored Infantry, and he was a patriot. He fought so the dream of America—life, liberty, and the pursuit of happiness—could be experienced by all.

Thankfully, the United States won the war against the Confederacy, but Black Americans, like Moses Davis, were still treated like second-class citizens in the country they fought for and died to unite. My ancestors were dehumanized in the country they built for free with their blood, sweat, and tears. The only payment they received was continued racism and structural systems that kept them oppressed. I applaud the White brothers and sisters in Christ who were abolitionists, like the British men William Wilberforce, John Wesley, and Charles Spurgeon. In a letter to the Black abolitionist Frederick Douglass, Spurgeon wrote,

I do from my inmost soul detest slavery . . . and although I commune at the Lord's table with men of all creeds, yet with a slave-holder I have no fellowship of any sort or kind. Whenever one has called upon me, I have considered it my duty to express my detestation of his wickedness, and I would as soon think of receiving a murderer into my church . . . as a man stealer.[1]

The great Frederick Douglass wrote,

We have men sold to build churches, women sold
to support the gospel, and babes sold to purchase
Bibles for the poor heathen! all for the glory of God
and the good of souls! The slave auctioneer's bell and
the church-going bell chime in with each other, and
the bitter cries of the heart-broken slave are drowned
in the religious shouts of his pious master. Revivals
of religion and revivals in the slave trade go hand in
hand.[2]

I love the pure, peaceable, and impartial Christianity
of Christ: I therefore hate the corrupt, slaveholding,
women-whipping, cradle-plundering, partial and
hypocritical Christianity of this land.[3]

Sadly, American Christianity is littered with White pastors
who supported slavery, legislated for policy that ensured slavery, owned slaves, and fought for segregation and Jim Crow
laws in the not-so-distant past. Some Christian denomina-
tions were even formed so that their members could own
slaves:

In 1845, when the American Baptist Foreign
Mission Society declared that any slave owner would
be disqualified from consideration for missionary
service, Baptist churches in the South seceded and

formed the Southern Baptist Convention so that
members would not have to choose between their
slaves and their calling to be missionaries.[4]

I am grateful that my Southern Baptist brothers and sisters have since formally denounced their initial stance on
slavery.

Richard Niebuhr, one of the preeminent authorities on
ethics and US church history, said nearly a century ago,
"Denominational divisions within the American Protestant
churches—which fell along racial, ethnic, and class lines—
were a glaring ethical failure." He went on to say that churches
of his day "accepted 'the accommodation of Christianity to
the caste system of human society.'" Niebuhr accurately com-
municated that "the division of the churches closely follows
the division of men into the caste of national, racial, and economic groups. It draws the color line in the church of God."
He also noted that nearly 90 percent of African American
Christians in the 1920s were members of Black denomina-
tions because of racism in the White church.[5]

Despite these historical facts, I am hopeful.

Why am I hopeful?

I am hopeful because Jesus rose from the dead.

And it is in the power of the Resurrection that you and I,
and all of God's beautifully color-blessed family, can simultaneously bring to light the sins of the church and our nation's
past and also recognize Jesus' victory over that sin, and all sin,
through the Cross.

An Invitation to the Conversation

I am often asked by my White brothers and sisters in Christ how they can help or what they can do as we work through this necessary revealing and healing process as the church and nation. We have to all recognize that this isn't a problem we can solve overnight, nor is there an easy fix. Instead, it begins with an invitation to the conversation. As we communicate together to create a gospel-shaped culture, there are some beginning points we need to be clear about. Here is what I would say to my White brothers and sisters.

First, when people of color who are your siblings in Christ bring up America's past atrocities and how Black people, other people of color, and poor Whites have been unjustly treated, remember that it does not mean we do not love America. It does not mean we do not take personal responsibility for our actions. It does not mean we are not grateful to be Americans. We love America so much so that we desire to see liberty and justice for all become more than a statement but a reality. As Christians, when that has not happened—or is not happening—we are moved to seek justice. We read in Proverbs,

> Speak up for those who cannot speak for themselves;
> ensure justice for those being crushed.
> Yes, speak up for the poor and helpless,
> and see that they get justice.
>
> PROVERBS 31:8-9, NLT

Second, your identity is in Christ Jesus, not in America. America's past injustices are not yours. Because your identity and self-worth are in Jesus, you can look back at the history of America and say, "Slavery, Jim Crow, Native American oppression, segregation, unjust housing laws, unjust policing, and other systems that have structurally oppressed people of color are wrong. In Christ, how do we collectively, as God's people, mourn the past and link arms in unity to never allow this to happen again?"

There is no reason for you to feel personally guilty about America's past structural injustices against people of color. But it is vital to healing the racial divide for you to see the larger historical landscape and the existence of the injustice. Baylor sociology professor George Yancey writes,

> While these majority group members did not directly participate in past racial sins, they have benefited from those sins. They enjoy their present economic standing partly because their ancestors were spared from racial discrimination. . . . Anyone who owns a home in the United States today and is not an Indian has benefited from the oppression of Native Americans. I do not make that statement to induce guilt, but it is a reality that we have to face.[6]

Third, as Americans, it is drilled into us that we can be anything we want to be if we just work hard enough. Acknowledging structural racial injustice does not mean that

White people have not worked hard. It simply means that the benefits of their hard work were not constrained by the color of their skin.

Can you imagine telling enslaved people in the 1800s, "You can be anything you want to be"?

Can you imagine telling Native Americans who have had their land, culture, and dignity brutally stolen, "You can be anything you want to be"?

Can you imagine telling my grandmother, who was born in 1932 in San Marcos, Texas, under the cruel fist of Jim Crow, "You can be anything you want to be"?

As a little boy, my grandmother would tell me how White police officers would beat and harass her father regularly. She told me how Black people could only rent or buy homes in certain parts of town, could only get certain jobs and attend certain schools. She was born into disadvantage because of the color of her skin. Not only was she called the N-word, but the structural racism all around her told her the same thing.

When issues like systemic racial injustice are brought up, I have found that my White brothers and sisters feel like this is a personal attack against their work ethic, self-worth, and way of being in the world. But that is not what I am saying at all! Instead, when I and others discuss systemic injustice, we are trying to open our eyes to recognize the historic limitations placed on Black Americans and people of color due to this form of oppression. In general, this has not been the situation for White people in America, although at specific times in the past, particular groups such as Italians, Eastern Europeans, and the Irish have encountered discrimination. Throughout American history, however, the racial caste framework has built monumental challenges into the systems of this nation for people of color. I am not saying that Black people and people of color today are not responsible for their individual actions. We *all* have a role to play in healing racial division and seeking to right the wrongs of the past.

Fourth, when a person of color brings up historic structural injustices, it is because history is a resource we can learn from—both the good and the bad. Can you imagine being diagnosed with lung cancer, and when the doctor asks you if you were a smoker, you said, "My past has nothing to do with your question; what is past is in the past"? The doctor is asking you about your past so she can understand why you are sick and suggest potential treatments—both negative behaviors to stop and positive behaviors to start.

Structural racism and injustices have played a major role, but not the only role, in creating the context we find ourselves in today. We need to diagnose the problem, see how the problem got us to where we are, and learn how we can collectively build bridges of grace instead of chasms of hate, mistrust, and indifference.

A garden will be overrun by weeds if we do not kill them at the root. Merely cutting a weed down is superficial. We must go deep into the soil and destroy the source. By looking at the past, we are identifying the root so we can kill it. Growing and maintaining a beautiful garden takes work.

This book is my attempt to do my part. I am praying millions will join me. Utopia is not possible, but as God's people, we are called to be a sign and foretaste of when "everything sad" will "come untrue."[7]

The Church Must Lead the Way

As you can see, there are plenty of difficult conversations that need to happen, and as color-blessed disciples, we should be leading the way. We must learn how to engage controversial issues from a posture of humility, unity, and oneness in Christ. As we saw in the previous chapter, there is no White supremacy or Black supremacy or any other supremacy; there is only the supremacy of Christ. We know that coming together will not be easy, but our unity in Christ compels us. Therefore, we must embrace tension in order to engage in difficult conversations that lead to healing.

One example of this sort of engagement is a long-standing partnership that exists between Transformation Church and the Charlotte-Mecklenburg Police Department. Throughout the past decade, policing and race have been a flash point in the community. Rather than being unengaged, Transformation Church has invited representatives of a variety of views to discuss the issue as brothers and sisters in Christ. In one of our Sunday morning conversations after a protest in Charlotte that escalated into violence, a young Black man who is a longtime member of our church and who marched in the protest shared some of his negative experiences with the police. He felt like the police viewed him as guilty and did not show him dignity. A police captain who is also a longtime member of our church shared the vetting process for potential police officers. He was also deeply disturbed by the police officers who were not acting in accordance with their calling. He wanted to get rid of bad police officers, but he also wanted to acknowledge the great work that good, hardworking police officers do every day. And finally, another longtime member of our church who is a judge shared his perspective of seeking justice and ruling fairly. I wanted our church to see how followers of Jesus, and members of the same local body, can have gospel-centered, humble conservations on hot-button issues. As the lead pastor of Transformation Church, I have to embody what I want my congregation to become.

Former CMPD chief of police Kerr Putney has spoken at our church several times over the years. As a pastor, one way I embrace the tension of our times is by discipling our church to be pro-police *and* pro–police reform. After the George Floyd murder that rocked the nation and led to widespread protests, I interviewed Chief Putney on Instagram Live. Here's some of what that discussion looked like:

> Me: Let me ask you this, Chief: When you saw the footage of what took place with George Floyd, is there any training in all of your years of experience where you've worked up the ranks to where you are now, that that is something that's taught to police officers?

Chief Putney: Absolutely not. When I saw the video, I was disgusted. It was the most cowardly act I've ever seen. It flies in the face of everything this profession wants to represent. And it hearkens back to all the history that you were speaking about that we've been struggling to overcome, to build trust and legitimacy to counter that narrative. And here we are dealing with that, again, in a way that just makes you sick to your stomach. . . .

Me: What practically can be done?

Chief Putney: Well, a lot of things. First of all, there's no perfect way to go about vetting people. They come in and just like you interviewing anybody for your company, or whatever else, they're going to present themselves one way. But we try to actually dig a little deeper. We do behavioral interviews, trying to see really what makes you tick, we look at your history, we look at your associates, we access your social media, we try to look for any signs and symptoms that might be explicit, specifically to your character and flaws in that character that would make you less than a good cop. And then when we put you through our training, we show you why we have such a high value on the sanctity of life. And we charge you with the responsibility of protecting it. And so we do a lot of things on the front end. . . . Legislation wise,

I wish there were a law or a rule or a directive or training—everybody talks about training, and I get it. We need more and more training to be better. We're a learning agency always trying to improve as most agencies around the country. But what you can't train is learned through your upbringing—your parents, I always say, give you the culture, they make you good people. We train you to be good cops. It starts with the former. You have to be a good person.[8]

As the church of Jesus Christ, we must lead the way in engaging controversial issues with the Kingdom of God guiding our values. But too often we allow political idolatry to distort our vision, blinding us to God's Kingdom and to unity with our brothers and sisters. There is no shortage of controversy in our society. Church leaders should be Spirit-led, discipling believers to engage with love and wisdom.

Where Do We Go from Here?

As we begin to have these difficult, culture-changing conversations, we can start to create something new. As Christians, we are empowered by the Holy Spirit to overcome the limitations of human division.

First, as God's multiethnic family, *we must understand and engage the real problem: sin and the dark powers of evil.*

White people are not the problem. Black people are not the problem. No single ethnic group is the problem. The problem is the seductive, destructive, and corruptive nature of sin. We are hopelessly broken beyond repair. We cannot fix ourselves. We need the Carpenter himself to fix us. He is the only one capable.

Until we dig out the root, we are going to keep cutting weeds, and the weeds are just going to keep growing. The world, as it is, is not the "very good" world God created. Humanity, the crown jewel of his creation, lived in *shalom*—harmony, peace, and wholeness with God and each other. But when our ancient parents Adam and Eve chose to live independently of the God who is life, they died spiritually, and sin entered creation and humanity.[9] They literally unleashed hell on earth.

Racism, along with other sins, attached itself to humanity like a parasite. Every person ever born, regardless of ethnicity, was born a sinner, corrupted to the core, devoid of God's life:

As the Scriptures say,

"No one is righteous—
    not even one.
No one is truly wise;
    no one is seeking God.
All have turned away;
    all have become useless.
No one does good,
    not a single one."
ROMANS 3:10-12, NLT

Every human being needs to be born again so the life that Adam and Eve lost can be restored to us. This is called regeneration. Those who trust Jesus, regardless of ethnicity, become participants in the triune God's life: "Yes, Adam's one sin brings condemnation for everyone, but Christ's one act of righteousness brings a right relationship with God and new life for everyone" (Romans 5:18, NLT).

Every human being born again in Jesus must grow so they can reflect his wisdom, compassion, love, mercy, and grace. This is called sanctification—the process of being made holy. Holiness is not something we do, but it is the work of God the Holy Spirit in us, making us more and more like Jesus as we surrender our fears, insecurities, doubts, prejudice, and hurts to him.

Spiritually immature followers of Jesus cannot fight racism or any other sin. It takes spiritual depth to uproot racism. It requires that we "build up the body of Christ, until we all reach unity in the faith and in the knowledge of God's Son, growing into maturity with a stature measured by Christ's fullness" (Ephesians 4:12-13).

Not only are human beings broken, but the powers of darkness use, abuse, and get humans under their control to do their evil bidding on earth, individually and through oppressive, unjust systems that govern society. The apostle Paul writes,

Once you were dead because of your disobedience and your many sins. You used to live in sin, just

like the rest of the world, obeying the devil—the
commander of the powers in the unseen world.
He is the spirit at work in the hearts of those
who refuse to obey God.

EPHESIANS 2:1-2, NLT

And also:

Put on the full armor of God so that you can stand
against the schemes of the devil. For our struggle is not
against flesh and blood, but against the rulers, against
the authorities, against the cosmic powers of this
darkness, against evil, spiritual forces in the heavens.

EPHESIANS 6:11-12

Dr. Anthony Bradley, professor of religious studies at the
King's College, helps us immensely to understand the various
ways sin affects our society:

Moreover, the devil is real and works through people
(Luke 8:29). Does racism exist in institutions and
structures in 2020? It depends. Because of the fall
and reality of the devil, it is not inconceivable to
believe that structures of sin exist but the evidence
will need to make that clear on a case-by-case
basis. Does white supremacy explain everything
that is wrong in America? No. Does racism explain
all racial struggles and racial disparities that

non-whites face in America? No. That view is overly simplistic, unsophisticated, and monistic. The world is too complex for one theory to explain all of the differentiated ways we see the implications of Genesis 3 reverberate throughout American culture where class and race intersect.[10]

Second, *we must learn to listen compassionately.* One of the greatest gifts you can give your brothers and sisters in Christ as we heal the racial divide is to listen to their stories with compassion. *Compassion* means "to suffer with." As we knit our hearts to Jesus' heart, he gives us the capacity to hear each other's hurts and enter each other's pain. When we truly start seeing each other as siblings, we can start listening compassionately to each other. To my White brothers and sisters, one of the most precious gifts you can give your siblings of color are these words: "I believe you. I am sorry that happened to you. I am for you. We are in this together."

Third, *we must learn to love extravagantly.* Jesus was an extravagant lover of God and people.

Love is acting in the face of fear on behalf of the one you love.

Love is sacrificial.

Love is consistent.

Our racial divide will ultimately be healed by White, Black, Asian, Latino, and Indigenous people who are committed to loving God and their siblings in Christ, who are not afraid to sacrifice, and who show up every day in the power of the Holy Spirit. Love must inform our conversations and our actions.

Fourth, *we must leverage our lives courageously as ambassadors of Messiah Jesus.* To leverage our lives for the betterment of another means to follow the pattern of Jesus, in the Spirit's power. Leveraging our lives in the Kingdom requires courage.

Courage is not the absence of fear.

Courage is you handing God your fear and God handing you his power.

Courage is you telling Jesus, "I can't. But I know you can."

Courage is learning new things and unlearning old things.

The dark powers of evil want to keep the racial divide in place. Those who have yet to be redeemed and regenerated or those who are immature or stubborn in their faith want to keep the racial divide in place.

This resistance does not matter, because Jesus is greater. In Christ Jesus, we are "more than conquerors" (Romans 8:37).

I believe he is looking for his people of all ethnicities to trust him and follow him. We must become extremists of love.

Love makes us courageous. Our Jewish Messiah, King Jesus, specializes in giving all his people courage.[11]

Jesus is inviting you into the often difficult but also fruitful conversation. By royal decree you have been summoned by the King. He wants to teach you how to love, listen, learn, and leverage your life for the sake of his gospel and his Kingdom.

| | | | | **MARINATE ON THIS** | | | |

PRAYER

Lord Jesus,
It took courage for you to go to the cross.
You became the bridge that connected us to the Father's love
*   by the Holy Spirit's presence.*
It was your shed blood that broke the back of sin and
*   the dark powers.*
It was your grace that unifies us in your Father's transcultural
*   family.*

Holy Spirit,
Give me the courage to be a unifier.
Give me the courage to seek understanding before seeking to
*   be understood.*
Give me the courage to unlearn things I need to and
*   to learn things I need.*

Father,
Make me an extremist of love.
Help me remember that love for my siblings in the
*   Messiah is committed, sacrificial, and*
*   consistent.*
May I mourn where I need to mourn.
May I take responsibility where I need to take
*   responsibility.*

Forgive me for my silence.
Make my life a voice of love.
Give me the grace to guard the unity King Jesus paid
*   such a high price to provide.*
Guide me in this ministry of reconciliation.
In Jesus' name,
Amen.

THINGS TO THINK ABOUT

- As followers of Jesus, we are "children of light" (Ephesians 5:8), exposing the darkness so healing, repentance, reconciliation, and restoration can occur.

- It is in the power of the Resurrection that you and I, and all of God's beautifully color-blessed family, can simultaneously bring to light the sins of the church and our nation's past and also recognize Jesus' victory over that sin, and all sin, through the Cross.

- There is no shortage of controversy in our society. Church leaders should be Spirit-led, discipling believers to engage with love and wisdom.

QUESTIONS TO DISCUSS

1. What has been your experience with the historical trauma that people of color have faced in the United States? Do you regularly have conversations about this topic with friends and family? If not, what's stopping you?

2. How do conversations help us work toward reconciliation? How can you listen compassionately to the pain and concerns of others?

3. "Our struggle is not against flesh and blood, but against the rulers, against the authorities, against the cosmic powers of this darkness, against evil, spiritual forces in the heavens" (Ephesians 6:12). The real problem in healing our racial divide is sin and demonic powers. How does this influence how we interact with those we disagree with? What is our role in engaging with the problem of sin and demonic powers?

GOSPEL BEHAVIORS TO PRACTICE

Spend time with a group of brothers and sisters in Christ of different ethnicities in prayer, mourning, listening, and learning. Set a date and time to make it a commitment.

CHAPTER 9

COLLECTIVELY MOURN INJUSTICE

Collectively, our eyes could not unsee the brutal, callous modern-day lynching of George Floyd by former Minneapolis Police officer Derek Chauvin. For over nine excruciating minutes, Mr. Floyd pleaded for his life as Chauvin's knee forced his neck to the street. Fellow police officers on the scene watched the murder in plain sight. They did nothing. Helpless people in the crowd pleaded for Chauvin to take his knee off Mr. Floyd's neck, but he would not. Mr. Floyd died. I am thankful Chauvin was found guilty of all three charges against him. He was sentenced to twenty-two and a half years in prison. There must be consequences for police brutality or it will continue. And I pray for Mr. Chauvin to meet Jesus, our forgiving King.

In an all-too-frequent scenario at Transformation Church since its beginning back in 2010, whether it was the White supremacist Dylann Roof mass murdering nine Black people at Mother Emanuel African Methodist Episcopal Church during a Bible study or another unarmed Black man being killed by a White officer under shady circumstances or a protest turned violent, my Sunday sermon opened with a time of mourning in response to the racial trauma. As the lead pastor of Transformation Church, it was vital that I lead and embody for our congregation the spiritual discipline of mourning. Racial trauma fueled by demonic powers reminds your Black siblings and other siblings of color of the historical injustices committed not so long ago. And collective mourning—regardless of your ethnicity—is the proper response.

What Is Mourning?

Mourning is not a word that modern Christians use much, but it is a biblical word that Jesus wants us to embrace and embody. King Jesus says, "Blessed are those who mourn, for they will be comforted" (Matthew 5:4). To mourn means to be heartbroken over the things that break God's heart. All sin breaks Jesus' heart. Stealing Native Americans' land breaks Jesus' heart. Selling human beings made in the image of God as property breaks Jesus' heart. Segregation and Jim Crow laws break Jesus' heart. Injustice of the past and present breaks Jesus' heart. "For I the LORD love justice; I hate robbery and injustice" (Isaiah 61:8).

Mourning is a holy longing, a loud cry of the soul that aches over the sad realities of our fallen world. Mourning is the *knowing* that one day sadness will be undone by Jesus. Mourning deepens our dependency on Jesus, the Suffering Servant. Mourning with others over injustice moves us toward loving what Jesus loves most—people. Truly loving others releases a great cry of mourning. When people we love hurt, we hurt too.

Perhaps you are wondering, especially if you are one of my White siblings in Christ, *Why would Derwin open his sermon with a time of mourning over a White police officer killing an unarmed Black man? There is violence all the time!*

First, to many Black Americans and people of color in general, the murder of George Floyd was a nine-minute reenactment of historical injustices. Over the years of serving Transformation Church, I have had many conversations with Black mothers and fathers and White parents who have adopted Black children or children of color who are fearful for their sons if they interact with police. Even in my own family, when my son and I were planning to drive from Hamilton, Montana, to Charlotte, my wife of thirty years, who is White, asked me, "Do you want me to go with you guys?" She asked because she had concern for us if we were pulled over.

I, along with other ministry leaders, have to disciple our people to "be strengthened by the Lord and by his vast strength," to "put on the full armor of God so that you can stand against the schemes of the devil. For our struggle is not against flesh and blood, but against the rulers, against the authorities, against the cosmic powers of this darkness, against evil, spiritual forces in the heavens" (Ephesians 6:10-12). And we have to teach others how to be understanding and compassionate siblings to those who are hurting. We are literally in this together.

Second, it is spiritual abuse and neglect of the pastoral calling for a pastor to be tone deaf from the pulpit when a national trauma occurs that triggers emotional wounds of a particular people group. How can we "carry one another's burdens" (Galatians 6:2) if those burdens are not talked about?

I do not subscribe to a theology of avoiding controversial topics. If I and other ministry leaders do not lead our people through controversial issues—from mass shootings, immigration, corporate greed, and abortion to racism, sexual ethics, political idolatry, and injustice—then late-night progressive or conservative news outlets will gladly do so, as they have done to great effect. I have found that many believers filter the "hot topics" of race and injustice through Democratic or Republican filters instead of theological filters. People will leave their churches over politics before they leave politics for a church. This morning as I was writing, I got word that two families left our church because I refuse to be pro-Republican. And I have had people leave our church because I refuse to be pro-Democrat. Political conservatives want me to wrap Jesus in an American flag, and political progressives want me to strip Jesus of ethics that do not fit their worldview. We leaders must address controversial topics through the redeeming work of Jesus so God's people can think and live in light of God's Kingdom.

Third, to my White siblings: your Black siblings in Christ remember sitting at dinner with their grandparents, being told stories of Black men lynched by police and White mobs. We watched documentaries about the Civil Rights Movement, in which police dogs were unleashed on Black people, tearing their flesh off for peacefully protesting. Black Americans, many of whom are followers of Jesus, simply wanted what the Constitution guaranteed them—the right to vote and participate in American democracy. The historical wounds of your Black siblings in Christ run deep, especially when the depth of our pain in the church and in our beloved America is often dismissed. Ponder the words of Dr. King as he describes these times in the not-so-distant past. The events he describes in "Letter from a Birmingham Jail" (August 1963) occurred not too many years before my birth in 1971:

> Birmingham is probably the most thoroughly
> segregated city in the United States. Its ugly record
> of police brutality is known in every section of this
> country. Its unjust treatment of Negroes in the
> courts is a notorious reality. There have been more
> unsolved bombings of Negro homes and churches
> in Birmingham than in any other city in this nation.
> These are the hard, brutal, and unbelievable facts.[1]

I am thankful that the United States and the church in America have come a long way. We should celebrate how far we have come. For example, in 1969, Dr. Tony Evans, one of my mentors from afar, "was told by the leadership of a large Southern Baptist church in Atlanta" that he was not welcome to worship there.[2] Today he headlines at Southern Baptist conferences. This is progress. But Jesus has so much more for us to take hold of.

Fourth, "the exposure to environments perceived as racist can result in an overactive physiological stress response. In other words, normal bodily systems responsible for adjusting to stressful conditions remain perpetually activated in the presence of chronic stress, leaving individuals vulnerable to illness due to elevated wear and tear on the body."[3] Strangely, as I write these words in Starbucks, my heart rate has increased, I am finding it hard to focus, and my anxiety levels have spiked. It reminds me of the constant awareness I have of being Black in America, and the transgenerational discrimination that I and people like me have experienced. My mind races back to a time when I was in Louisiana at a bass fishing tournament when a White guy yelled, "White power!" as I walked past him in the bathroom. Thoughts of being at church conferences throughout the years where Black theologians and preachers and preachers of color in general were talked about as though their ministries and theology were inadequate compared to their White siblings'. I cannot allow that pain to be greater than the redemptive work of Jesus. The pain is not greater than the Cross. And so we must confront racism in our churches for the sake of our siblings in Christ.

To my beloved White siblings in Christ Jesus, it is a

spiritual discipline and an act of immense love to mourn with us, to enter our experience, and to embrace us in solidarity against the forces of darkness. Marinate on this:

> The health consequences of racism and discrimination can be persistent and passed from one generation to the next through the body's "biological memory" of harmful experiences. . . . Stressful conditions and poor health experienced by mothers can lead to alterations in her offspring's gene expression without changing his or her genotype. These changes in gene expression can have important implications for the healthy functioning of bodily systems in mothers and their offspring.[4]

And to my Black siblings and other siblings of color, our spiritual formation and commitment to walk in the power of the Spirit is essential. There is never going to be a world where sin is eradicated until Jesus returns and ushers in the new heaven and the new earth. Therefore, our mutual exchange of grace, compassion, friendship, and love is vital to our flourishing. Our "in this togetherness" is crucial to cohealing the racial divide through the crucified and risen Messiah.

Finally, mourning injustice that does not impact you but affects your sibling in Christ of another ethnicity creates intimacy and deepens bonds of love. Intimacy—"into-me-you-see"—is a gift. It is a gift of siblingship to cry with your brother or sister, to hurt when they hurt, to have solidarity with them in their pain, and to desire the Jesus-kind-of-justice to fill the earth.

When you and I sit with someone in their pain, our presence is a gift. On May 17, 2004, Vicki, my bride and best friend, was diagnosed with thyroid cancer. Surgery was required to remove the cancerous tumor. We left for the hospital early in the morning. While I was sitting in the hospital waiting room, a doctor who was an elder of the church we were members of saw me and prayed with me. Friends came to the hospital all day long to check on us. But one family, the Scurlocks, arrived early in the morning. People came and went all day, but they, along with their young children, stayed the whole day. They did not say much to me, but their presence in our pain spoke the love of Jesus loudly. They mourned with us. And in their sharing of our pain, we gained new levels of intimacy that stretch to this very day.

When White siblings mourn with their Black siblings and siblings of color because of racism and injustice, greater depths of love are forged. And demonic powers hate when we love each other. There must be a mutual exchange of our love, and this is embodied in mourning.

What Does Collective Mourning Look Like?

On the Sunday after Mr. Floyd was murdered, I led our people through a short historical narrative of the Black community and policing. As you read in the previous chapter, at Transformation Church, we love and respect the men and women in blue. But equally, we must engage in an honest assessment of historical injustice. Once again, like me, you can be pro-police *and* pro–police reform—unless you think that somehow policing is not affected by "total depravity" and the dark demonic powers the way everything else in creation is.

So what does collective mourning look like? Collective mourning includes four reminders.

First, collective mourning reminds the family of Abraham to corporately pray. In corporate prayer, the body of Christ— the people baptized and clothed in Christ—is reminded of our inheritance, a glorious future in the new heaven and new earth where mourning does not exist. In the fully redeemed, colorful family that God promised Abraham, we will rejoice in the Lamb of God. Tomorrow's hope is today's power:

> For the Lamb who is at the center of the throne
> will shepherd them;
> he will guide them to springs of the waters of life,
> and God will wipe away every tear from their eyes.
> REVELATION 7:17

Second, collective mourning reminds the family of Abraham to name the injustice we are mourning. There cannot be healing without revealing. When you go to a doctor because you are sick, she will ask you for your symptoms, check your vitals, run tests, and find out what is wrong with you. If the doctor does not know what your illness is, you will get a misdiagnosis, stay sick, get sicker, or die. The church is sick. As I showed in the last chapter, in many historical instances, America and the church have perpetuated heinous racism and injustice. Once again, you and I can deeply love our country and our churches *and* be concerned over the ugly things that have taken and are taking place. In the last chapter, sadly, you saw that the church in many instances has sided with taking Native Americans' land, slavery, segregation, and Jim Crow laws. Regrettably, the church has not led the way in racial reconciliation. How sad! We are the people who have the cure to the sickness: "You have been united with Christ Jesus. Once you were far away from God, but now you have been brought near to him through the blood of Christ" (Ephesians 2:13, NLT).

We need to name this illness, mourn it, and repent of the ways we have been silent, complicit, or indifferent. We are not responsible for the sins of our forefathers, but we are responsible to mourn and undo their damage as best we can. This is basic Christianity. Mourning the sins of our forefathers may seem strange in American Christianity, but it is a normative spiritual discipline in the Bible. Ponder the words of the prophet Nehemiah:

> When I heard these words, I sat down and wept. I mourned for a number of days, fasting and praying before the God of the heavens. I said,
>
> > LORD, the God of the heavens, the great and awe-inspiring God who keeps his gracious

covenant with those who love him and keep his commands, let your eyes be open and your ears be attentive to hear your servant's prayer that I now pray to you day and night for *your servants, the Israelites.* I confess the sins *we* have committed against you. *Both I and my father's family* have sinned. *We* have acted corruptly toward you and have not kept the commands, statutes, and ordinances you gave your servant Moses. Please remember what you commanded your servant Moses: "If you are unfaithful, I will scatter you among the peoples. But if you return to me and carefully observe my commands, even though your exiles were banished to the farthest horizon, I will gather them from there and bring them to the place where I chose to have my name dwell." *They* are your servants and your people. You redeemed *them* by your great power and strong hand. Please, Lord, let your ear be attentive to the prayer of your servant and to that of your servants who delight to revere your name.

NEHEMIAH 1:4-11, EMPHASIS ADDED

Note how Nehemiah's mourning has a corporate dimension of repentance. He is asking for forgiveness on behalf of other Israelites—he is mourning their sin and desiring for Israel to obey God and to corporately undo the damage caused by their corporate sin. We must individually ask for forgiveness to receive its effects, but we can mourn sin committed by our past and present family members. Just think of the Lord's Prayer, which is prayed collectively, in plural: "Forgive *us our* sins, as *we* have forgiven those who sin against *us*" (Matthew 6:12, NLT, emphasis added).

Third, collectively mourning reminds the family of Abraham of our unity in Christ. In a beautiful mystery, the crucified, resurrected Messiah, through the promised Holy Spirit, clothes and unites the Jew, the Indigenous, the White, the Black, the Asian, and the Latino in Christ. We are plunged into the Messiah, forever united to him and to each other, "for those of you who were baptized into Christ have been clothed with Christ. There is no Jew or Greek, slave or free, male and female; since you are all one in Christ Jesus" (Galatians 3:27-28).

Paul says, "All the members [of Christ's body] care for each other. If one part suffers, all the parts suffer with it, and if one part is honored, all the parts are glad" (1 Corinthians 12:25-26, NLT). Suffering with your siblings is a gift and a calling.

Fourth, collectively mourning reminds the family of Abraham that we are called into holiness. As we mourn injustice corporately, we are reminded that we are the body of Christ, the multicolored hands and feet of Jesus, his ambassadors of reconciliation.[5] Those of us colorfully clothed in Christ Jesus, sealed and filled by the Spirit, are eager to partner with Jesus in righting wrongs, healing hurts, and bringing justice into the chaos of injustice. The late John Stott writes,

If we love our neighbor as God made him, we must inevitably be concerned for his total welfare, the good of his soul, his body and his community. . . . Which means the quest for better social structures in which peace, dignity, freedom and justice are secured for all men. . . . The gospel lacks visibility if we merely preach it, and lacks credibility if we who preach it are interested only in souls and have no concern about the welfare of people's bodies, situations and communities.[6]

Through our union with Jesus, who "gave his life to free us from every kind of sin, to cleanse us, and to make us his very own people, totally committed to doing good deeds" (Titus 2:14, NLT), we mourn, and we also pursue justice as we pursue holiness. Mourning is oxygen to the lungs of mission and justice.

What Happens When We Corporately Mourn?

I know that anytime I enter the rushing waters of racism or injustice, the heat of spiritual warfare intensifies to scalding temperatures. No matter how gospel-drenched the mourning and sermon are, a few responses will be negative. In each of the negative responses, I and other ministry leaders try to have clarifying conversations. Some of these conversations are healing and restorative. Some end with people leaving our church. It always hurts when people leave.

However, for every negative response, there are many more positive responses. Here is a response of gratefulness from a White sister that is a member of our church:

> If it happens in the world, we feel it at Transformation Church. It's part of our spiritual formation. It comes with diversity. Racism, political divides, COVID, immigration, pro-life, loving our neighbor, injustice. We talk about it, regularly. It is not "getting political." But we explore it through the lens of Scripture, not a political platform. Grateful.

Our collective mourning is a spiritual discipline that forms us collectively into the image of Christ. Entering pain that was not inflicted upon you is a great measure of maturity that blesses your brothers and sisters who are suffering.

Research shows that for White Americans, their notion of race and fairness is shaped by their everyday experiences, which are different from those of Black Americans and people of color. For White Americans, their interactions are shaped primarily by other White people. It becomes an echo chamber. As Robert P. Jones writes, "Despite the demise of Jim Crow laws and race-restrictive housing ordinances, and the rise of integrated workplaces, white Americans' most meaningful relationships are almost exclusively with other white people."[7] Echo chambers of homogeneity morph into cages that limit our capacity to empathize and mourn.

When our neighborhoods and churches lack ethnic

diversity or when we just do not attempt to connect with the "other," White Christians do not interact at a deep level with people who might challenge what they think is normal or what their cable news station is telling them.[8] True, gospel-shaped spaces where brothers and sisters of different ethnicities can collectively mourn (such as multiethnic churches) are vital to our discipleship and enhance Jesus' mission to make disciples of all people.[9] When we mourn together, we grow in intimacy and go into the world together as one. Jennifer Harvey writes,

> Whites tend to become deeply invested in racial justice and anti-racism work only after they become invested in the lives of people of color through experiencing long-term, meaningful relationships. The power and impact of structural and personal racism, and passive white tolerance of these, become more visceral for whites when we see how real these are in the life of someone for whom we care.[10]

There is power in corporate mourning. When God's family prays for one another, cries with one another, and commits to a more just future together, we forge these "long-term, meaningful relationships" where real healing can happen. The beauty of this reality is reflected in an email I received from a White member of Transformation Church:

Pastor Derwin,

I didn't know what my Black friends went through until I adopted two Black children. When these two precious kids entered our life, it was like we entered a different America. I saw how differently they were treated than my White children. I saw how in stores they were followed and profiled. I saw how they were stopped for driving while Black. My husband and I asked a Black member of Transformation Church to have "the talk" with our sons about what to do when being pulled over by a policeman. It was painful. It was exhausting. There is a sense of weight I carry all day long now.

Thank you for providing a church like Transformation Church where we have community, solidarity, role models, but most importantly, Jesus and his gospel.

As we mourn sins of the past and the present, God's presence becomes a comforting gift that binds us together, unifying us deeper in him.

MARINATE ON THIS

PRAYER

Father,

Give me a heart that mourns the pain of past and present injustices.

Give me a love that cries and prays with my brothers and sisters who are in pain.

Lord Jesus,

You entered our world of injustice to show us what justice looks like clothed in humanity.

Through the Holy Spirit's power, live justly in me and through me for your glory,

the good of my siblings, and a world that does not know our Savior.

May our love for one another show the world Jesus.

Amen.

THINGS TO THINK ABOUT

- Mourning is a holy longing, a loud cry of the soul that aches over the sad realities of our fallen world. Mourning is the *knowing* that one day sadness will be undone by Jesus. Mourning deepens our dependency on Jesus, the Suffering Servant. Mourning with others over injustice moves us toward loving what Jesus loves most—people.

- Mourning injustice that does not impact you but affects your sibling in Christ of another ethnicity creates intimacy and deepens bonds of love. Intimacy—"into-me-you-see"—is a gift. It is a gift of siblingship to cry with your brother or sister, to hurt when they hurt, to have solidarity with them in their pain, and to desire the Jesus-kind-of-justice to fill the earth.

- True, gospel-shaped spaces where brothers and sisters of different ethnicities can collectively mourn (such as multiethnic churches) are vital to our discipleship and enhance Jesus' mission to make disciples of all people. When we mourn together, we grow in intimacy and go into the world together as one.

QUESTIONS TO DISCUSS

1. "Mourning is not a word that modern Christians use much" (page 194). Why do you think that is? Why is it important to recover this concept as we seek to heal our racial divide?

2. Why is it important to mourn past sins that we ourselves did not commit? How can you and your church model this collective mourning?

3. Think of a time when you experienced sorrow. What was helpful to you in that time? Who came alongside you and helped you? How do your past experiences of sorrow shed light on how you might collectively mourn injustice with your siblings in Christ of another ethnicity?

GOSPEL BEHAVIORS TO PRACTICE

This week, read or watch the news from another news source than the one you typically use. What pains and sorrows do you see that you might have overlooked otherwise? Instead of skipping over stories that don't seem to affect you, try to put yourself in the position of the people in pain, and mourn. Cry out to God against injustice and pray for a time when "God will wipe away every tear from their eyes" (Revelation 7:17).

CHAPTER 10

DISPLAY GOSPEL CHARACTER

After I played for the Indianapolis Colts from 1993 to 1997, my family moved to Charlotte, North Carolina, when I joined the Carolina Panthers. Now that I was in a new city, I needed to find a new barber. A few of my teammates told me about Gordon's barbershop.

The Black barbershop is a cultural experience where philosophers and poets pontificate on sports, religion, politics, and just about everything else. It's a weekly event you await with expectation. I met Gordon, a big, loud, boisterous man, and as soon as I saw him, I knew God had given me the assignment of reaching him with the gospel.

Over the months, we became friends. Gordon made it

213

clear he didn't care much for White people. As an older Black man, he had experienced racism personally and remembered the fight for civil rights. In his hurt, he painted an entire group of people with a broad brush of dislike. Religiously, he was a mixture of Nation of Islam and fragments of Christianity. He would try to tear down my faith by saying Christianity was a "White man's religion." God called me to be patient and kind with him in the way the Lord was patient and kind with me.

One time when we were playing golf together, Gordon hit his white golf ball into the woods. He was so desperate to beat me that he walked into the woods to find his ball. After several minutes, he came out with a pink golf ball, saying, "I found my ball!"

I said, "Gordon, you have a pink golf ball. You were using a white one." I started laughing, but he insisted he was using a pink golf ball the whole time. That was Gordon—loud, ornery, and prideful.

But then the life Gordon had built on sand started to collapse. His wife was diagnosed with breast cancer, and he experienced personal disappointments and setbacks. In the middle of this storm, he met the one who still quiets storms. He met Jesus. His life was transformed. His pride was swallowed up by humility, his meanness melted into kindness, and his prejudice toward White people turned into gracism. He was still loud and boastful, but now he was loud and boastful for Jesus. His barbershop turned into his pulpit.

I wrote a note on the inside cover of the Bible I gave him

in 1999. For two decades, he read his Bible so much that he had to duct-tape it to keep it from falling apart. As his Bible eventually came to pieces, he framed the note I wrote him. It looked like papyrus:

Gordon,
   I am so honored that Jesus brought me into your life. You were once empty and mean. You are now growing in the love of Jesus Christ. You are a new man in Christ Jesus. I know that God is going to use you in a mighty way. Enjoy the Bible; meditate on it day and night.

In Christ,
Derwin

The God of heaven and earth saves, transforms, and moves his people in the direction of loving all people. Becoming holy means becoming a lover of people.

Gordon changed when he met Jesus. He became more like the person he followed. When we are disciples of Jesus, we change too. The Holy Spirit molds us so that we are shaped by gospel character.

Early in my journey with Jesus, Colossians 1:28-29 was presented as a key text of discipleship: "We proclaim [Jesus], warning and teaching everyone with all wisdom, so that we may present everyone mature in Christ. I labor for this, striving with his strength that works powerfully in me."

This text is powerful. God wants his people to *mature*.

This teaching means that our lives are shaped to reflect Jesus. It is the power of God in us that accomplishes this act of grace as we give him more access to our sins, our hurts, our fears, our disappointments, and our insecurities. But this text becomes even more powerful when we realize that Paul was writing to a multiethnic congregation and teaching them how to love each other.[1]

Paul was suffering for proclaiming a gospel that reconciles people to God and each other across ethnic barriers. The mystery that Paul spoke of is that the "Gentiles are coheirs, members of the same body, and partners in the promise in Christ Jesus through the gospel" (Ephesians 3:6).

This is the beautiful struggle. In our differences and learning to put down our preferences and pick up our crosses, we grow and mature in gospel character. The mystery is that Christ the King lives in his multicolored family so we can love each other.

Third Race

In the summer of 2020, I found myself in a sea of peaceful people, protesting police brutality and racial injustice. The crowd at this Black Lives Matter (BLM) protest was ethnically and generationally diverse—a medley of Black, White, Latino, and Asian people, unified for a common cause. The crowd resembled Transformation Church—a mixture of young and old and swirls of different colors. I thought, *Why is a BLM protest more diverse than the church in America? This sort of diversity should be the composition of every church in America where demographics make it possible.*

The church remains deeply segregated in America. Christians of different ethnicities are increasingly divided. We read the same Bible, but we experience America differently. Researcher Ed Stetzer writes that American churchgoers "like the idea of diversity. They just don't like being around different people."[2] Seventy-one percent of evangelicals say their church is diverse enough.[3] Regrettably, American churches are ten times more segregated than the neighborhoods they are in and twenty times more segregated than nearby schools.[4] Echo chambers of segregation and disunity reinforce ethnic division, intensify political division, breed inequality, and foster injustice.[5] The implications of the segregated church in America stifle the mission of God, hinder discipleship, and display a divided church. This segregation does not reflect the character of Jesus that Christians are called to display.

The Lord knew if we were to remain isolated in our ethnic ghettos of sameness, we would not experience the unity he died and rose again to achieve. Our ethnic and cultural isolation is to our own peril. The power of the "other" educates and adds value to our lives if we are willing to have a mutual exchange of life in the gospel.

The apostle Paul wrote to the Corinthian church,

Some of us are Jews, some are Gentiles, some are slaves, and some are free. But we have all been baptized into one body by one Spirit, and we all share the same Spirit. Yes, the body has many different parts, not just one part. If the foot says, "I am not a part of the body because I am not a hand," that does not make it any less a part of the body. And if the ear says, "I am not part of the body because I am not an eye," would that make it any less a part of the body? If the whole body were an eye, how would you hear? Or if your whole body were an ear, how would you smell anything?

1 CORINTHIANS 12:13-17, NLT

Paul reminds this church—and us—that to ignore, dismiss, and not want to learn from the other parts of Jesus' body shrinks our capacity to be disciples. Hence a secular organization like BLM can be more diverse than the church in America.

No, I am not a member of BLM or an advocate of BLM. However, BLM did something Jesus' followers should have been doing—raising awareness of the racial injustice Black people and people of color, in general, have experienced individually and systemically in America. N. T. Wright comments,

Secular modernism has tried to get the fruits of the Jesus-message without the roots. It can't be done. Christianity was the original multicultural society, committed to caring for the poor and to sharing a common life across racial boundaries. Trying to recreate a society like that without Jesus leading the way is like trying to type with your fingers tied together.[6]

The historic Black church and gospel-shaped advocates like Dr. John Perkins (whose story we'll look at in the next chapter) have been leading in this cause, waiting for the majority of our White siblings to join us. A secular organization cannot bring into being what the multicolored, Spirit-indwelled body of Christ was left on earth to do.

One of the most compelling realities of Jesus' saving work is that his grace creates a new race. A new race walked out of the tomb with Jesus.[7] To see your Jewish, White, Black, Asian, Indigenous, and Latino brothers and sisters is to see Jesus.

The term *third race* is alluded to in 1 Peter 2:9. Peter, the one Paul had to confront in Antioch for the sin of racism, says that Jews and Gentiles in the Messiah are a new, "chosen race [*genos eklekton*]." Though we are different colors with diverse cultures, the red blood of King Jesus runs through our veins, making us family. Clement of Alexandria, a theologian in the second century, wrote, "We who worship God in a new way, as the third race, are Christians."[8] In Christ, as God's new people, we are participants in his new creation, a community of unity that exists to display his new society of love.

The first Christians were like us twenty-first-century

Christians in that we are new creations in Christ but not yet fully sanctified. Therefore, we hold on to old patterns of thinking about people that are beneath the gospel. Paul was on a mission to get the Jews and Gentiles to understand the bigness of God's grace and their place in his family. Even in Paul's churches, Jews thought they were ethnically and culturally superior to Gentiles, and Gentiles thought of themselves as ethnically and culturally superior to Jews. How did he go about the sacred task of unfolding the bigness of God's grace so they could learn to be family? He taught them about the new race of grace. And this teaching will help us as we seek to display gospel character in our lives today.

This New Race of Grace Shares Jesus' Life

I love the relationship between my adult son and daughter as they vibe together in unity. But it was not always this way. When my daughter hit her teen years and my son was around nine, they would pick at each other. My wife and I would constantly remind them, "You are blood. Love each other!"

Paul did something similar with the congregation in Ephesus when he wrote, "The church is his body; it is made full and complete by Christ, who fills all things everywhere with himself" (Ephesians 1:23, NLT). Ethnic disunity in the body of Christ is like a school of piranhas eating themselves. Jesus' body is Latino, Asian, White, Black, and Indigenous. This is serious gospel business. For too long preachers have preached the Bible too individualistically, and we have read it asking, "What's in it for me?" instead of asking, "What has Jesus accomplished so the *me* can be included in the *we* for God's glory?"

All those in the body of Jesus were at one time spiritually dead. Humanity's problem is not sin but spiritual death. According to Paul, spiritually dead people are born under the influence of demonic powers; even our good efforts are tainted by sin.[9] We all need to be born again. King Jesus wants to make us alive with his life, experiencing God's presence, purpose, and power. He freed us from the dark powers of evil, death, and sin. Regardless of our ethnicity, apart from Christ, we are separated from the presence and life of God, under the tyranny of our sin nature.

But God, who is rich in mercy and who loves us with unending, life-giving love, raises his children to life with Jesus. The same Jesus who walked out of that dark tomb is alive, walking in his colorful family. We all come to Jesus the same way: as spiritually dead, doomed people in need of God's mercy and resurrection life. Grace is a person, and his name is Jesus. His claim to fame is that he is the eternal Son of God, the Savior-King of Jews and Gentiles. He seats his people in the heavens with him and walks with them on earth.[10] When you and I understand the epicness of God's mercy and the incredible richness of his grace, the mere thought of being racist, or indifferent toward racial injustice, will be recognized as cosmic treason against Jesus.

This New Race of Grace Is Characterized by *Humility*

For Paul, the Cross bridged the ancient, sinful social boundaries of ethnicity, class, and gender to form a countercultural community that was unrivaled in the Roman Empire. Rome and all its wealth and military power could not reproduce the unity of the first Christians. The gospel levels the playing field. No one can boast in their own works to become acceptable to God through appeasing him with their moral performance. No one can boast in their ethnicity as God's favorites. We all enter God's family by grace through faith in Christ alone:

> This righteousness is given through faith in Jesus
> Christ to all who believe. There is no difference
> between Jew and Gentile, for all have sinned and fall
> short of the glory of God, and all are justified freely by
> his grace through the redemption that came by Christ
> Jesus. . . . Where, then, is boasting? It is excluded. . . .
> For we maintain that a person is justified by faith
> apart from the works of the law. Or is God the God
> of Jews only? Is he not the God of Gentiles too? Yes,
> of Gentiles too, since there is only one God, who will
> justify the circumcised by faith and the uncircumcised
> through that same faith.
>
> ROMANS 3:22-24, 27-30, NIV

Jews and Gentiles—you and me—are rescued from the kingdom of darkness and brought into the kingdom of light by grace through faith in the Messiah alone. The ethnic badges of this new race of grace are faith and baptism. Members of this new race of grace "are all children of God through faith in Christ Jesus. And all who have been united with Christ in baptism have put on Christ, like putting on new clothes" (Galatians 3:26-27, NLT). We boast in Jesus alone, not in our ethnicity or moral performance. Paul writes,

> As for me, may I never boast about anything except the cross of our Lord Jesus Christ. Because of that cross, my interest in this world has been crucified, and the world's interest in me has also died. It doesn't matter whether we have been circumcised or not. What counts is whether we have been transformed into a new creation.
>
> GALATIANS 6:14-15, NLT

Humility characterizes the heart of color-blessed disciples because we recognize that we are saved by grace, through faith, not because of who we are or what we've done. The Good News of Jesus gives us eyes to see ourselves and other people—regardless of ethnicity, class, or gender—without envy or superiority, as image-bearers of God.

This New Race of Grace Is Characterized by *Reconciliation*

When I first met Jesus, I was infatuated with what he had done for me. It was me, Jesus, and my Bible. But the more

I read, the more I learned that the Bible is about Jesus, his church, and his mission to make all things new. Just as Paul told the first Christians, we are adopted into Abba's family, and in Christ, we are God's *workmanship*. We become his paintbrushes, and creation becomes the canvas in which he uses our redeemed colors and cultures to create the beauty of his Kingdom on earth: "We are his workmanship, created in Christ Jesus for good works, which God prepared ahead of time for us to do" (Ephesians 2:10).

God gives us grace so that his people can produce good works that he "prepared ahead of time for us to do." What are these "good works"? Glad you asked. Paul tells us:

> So, then, remember that at one time you were
> Gentiles in the flesh. . . . At that time you were
> without Christ, excluded from the citizenship of
> Israel, and foreigners to the covenants of promise,
> without hope and without God in the world. But
> now in Christ Jesus, you who were far away have
> been brought near by the blood of Christ.
> EPHESIANS 2:11-13

The "good works" are reconciliation with God and reconciliation with others. Jesus spilled his blood on the cross to get Jews ("those who were near") and Gentiles (those "who were far away") to be brought close to God and to each other (Ephesians 2:17). All of this was in alignment with the covenantal promise to Abraham long ago. Ethnic reconciliation through the gospel is important to God.

This New Race of Grace Is Characterized by *Peace*

Because we come from different backgrounds and experiences, we see the world in diverse ways. These differences can cause conflict, but they can also cause awareness and awakening to a new way to look at things.

A few months ago, I was on the *ChurchPulse Weekly* podcast hosted by Carey Nieuwhof and Brooke Hempell. Before we started recording, Carey mentioned that he knew how much I love to fish. He said, "Derwin, in 1789, when the French came to Ontario, it was reported that the lakes had so many fish you could walk on the backs of fish from canoe to canoe. Wouldn't you love to travel back and fish here?"

I said, "No way, man, 1789 was not a good time to be a Black man in North America." We laughed.

Then Carey said, "Derwin, I'm so sorry. I've never thought about it from a Black person's perspective."

"Carey," I responded, "no need to apologize. We are siblings in Christ, called to love and teach each other." In love, I was able to open Carey's eyes to see a reality that he had not seen because his point of reference as a White Canadian was different from mine.

Jesus brings peace to his diverse and divided family through his shed blood. His blood gives us peace with his

Abba and with each other. Peace, unity, and reconciliation are gifts included in our salvation the moment we are incorporated into Jesus' body. We do not have to create them; Jesus' blood has already done that. Through the indwelling life of Jesus, we must "get rid of all bitterness, rage, anger, harsh words, and slander, as well as all types of evil behavior" (Ephesians 4:31, NLT) and walk by faith in the peace that he has already provided: "For Christ himself has brought peace to us. He united Jews and Gentiles into one people when, in his own body on the cross, he broke down the wall of hostility that separated us" (Ephesians 2:14, NLT).

Paul, a master teacher, reminds Jews and Gentiles of the Temple in Jerusalem and how the Gentiles could only gather in the outer courts. There was a wall that separated them from the inner courts, where only the Jews could enter. When Jesus accomplished salvation, his body on the cross tore down the dividing wall.[11] This was a physical tearing and a spiritual tearing. In Christ, unity is *accomplished* by the blood and body of Jesus. He dismantled, brick by brick, the wall of sin that separates us from God and from each other. Jesus' body is the place where we come together in the bond of peace. In the gospel of Christ Jesus, cast aside your stereotypes, prejudices, and fears. Hostility was put to death by Jesus. It is finished. Walk in his power of reconciliation.

Jesus "create[ed] in himself one new people" from Jews and Gentiles (Ephesians 2:15, NLT). The Greek term for "new" (*kainos*) means "new in kind." The people of God are not Jews or Gentiles, but the new people of God (Christians, a family of

Jews and Gentiles, just as God promised Abraham).[12] Our colors and cultures are celebrated and enhanced. We are blessed with unity in diversity. It is time that we grow up, obey Christ, and walk in unity. We must refuse to allow our fears, demons, and social and political culture of division to rip us apart. We are the body of Christ. We must, by faith, "make every effort to keep [our]selves united in the Spirit, binding [our]selves together with peace" (Ephesians 4:3, NLT).

This New Race of Grace Is Characterized by Being a *Living Temple*

For the Gentiles, the pagan temples were where their gods dwelled. For the Jews, the Jewish Temple was where the living God of heaven was present. Paul makes an epic gospel claim when he says,

> Now all of us can come to the Father through the
> same Holy Spirit because of what Christ has done
> for us. So now you Gentiles are no longer strangers
> and foreigners. You are citizens along with all of
> God's holy people. You are members of God's family.
> Together, we are his house, built on the foundation
> of the apostles and the prophets. And the cornerstone
> is Christ Jesus himself. We are carefully joined
> together in him, becoming a holy temple for the Lord.
> Through him you Gentiles are also being made part
> of this dwelling where God lives by his Spirit.
> EPHESIANS 2:18-22, NLT

A gospel-shaped understanding of multiethnic reconciliation is rooted in Jesus giving all of us access to the Father. Through the unrivaled redemptive work of Jesus, his multiethnic church is now the temple where heaven and earth meet. Each multicolored person is a brick in God's temple, bearing his image.

When we meet Jesus, he transforms us. But this transformation is not just for ourselves. It is so we can be good brothers and sisters to our siblings in Christ. Grace creates a new race of grace. And this new race leans into the Holy Spirit's power so we can worship Jesus by loving our siblings in Christ.

Love Is Colorful

A young Black family started attending Transformation Church and then became members. Eventually, they joined the small group that my wife and I were in. Our small group resembled our church—ethnically, generationally, and socioeconomically diverse. After a few months, the father told me, "This is the first time I have trusted and loved White people. With my past interactions, I did not think that would ever happen." His wife had grown up in an area where she experienced police harassment and had been called the N-word more times than she could count. She mentioned, "I would have never imagined being in a church with White people. And I trust them to take care of my children. Jesus has transformed me through this church."

I had an older White woman in our church grab my hand after service and say, "Pastor, I love you. Growing up as a little girl, my only interactions with Black people were the help around the house. God is using you and this church to help me see things I've never seen before. Thank you for being my pastor."

Proximity creates intimacy ("into-me-you-see"). Sharing our hurts, our disappointments, our fears, and our victories binds us together.

Paul gives us the blueprint for intimacy in Romans 12:9-16. The blood-bought, reconciled, forgiven mosaic called the church is to "love . . . without hypocrisy." We are to cling to the goodness of God's Kingdom. Our love for each other must be deep and sacrificial, honoring the image of God in each of us. Love is hopeful, selfless, patient in times of distress, and graceful in moments of conflict. This divinely generated love refuses vengeance but is gracious to and laments with siblings when they hurt. The love God created us to enjoy is harmonious, humble, life-giving, and forgiving. Worship is the color of love that pursues peacemaking, because peacemakers "will be called the children of God" (Matthew 5:9, NLT), overcoming evil with good.

We cannot love like this. It is beyond us. But this kind of love is not beyond Jesus. It is *from* Jesus. Give Jesus your fears, prejudices, and pride. He will love through you.

The racial divide is healed by people who allow Jesus to love through them, which is what displaying gospel character looks like.

| | | | **MARINATE ON THIS** | | | |

PRAYER

Father,
Regardless of our ethnicity, class, or gender,
we were dead, doomed, and separated from you and
*   each other.*
But you overflow with mercy and love us with an
*   everlasting love*
that is life-giving and sin-forgiving.
You sent Jesus as a gift of grace.

King Jesus,
Your grace is more amazing than I realize.
Your grace is bigger and better than I know.
Give me eyes to see your grace so I can experience what it
*   did for me*
and how it included me in your Father's family.

Holy Spirit,
I, along with my multicolored siblings, am the dwelling
*   place of the Most High God.*
May we love each other as Jesus loved us, sacrificially.
We are the body of Jesus, a wondrous mosaic, a new race
*   of grace.*
Amen.

THINGS TO THINK ABOUT

- Though we are different colors with diverse cultures, the red blood of King Jesus runs through our veins, making us family. In Christ, as God's new people, we are participants in his new creation, a community of unity that exists to display his new society of love.

- Humility characterizes the heart of color-blessed disciples because we recognize that we are saved by grace, through faith, not because of who we are or what we've done. The Good News of Jesus gives us eyes to see ourselves and other people—regardless of ethnicity, class, or gender—without envy or superiority, as image-bearers of God.

- In Christ, unity is *accomplished* by the blood and body of Jesus. He dismantled, brick by brick, the wall of sin that separates us from God and from each other. Jesus' body is the place where we come together in the bond of peace.

QUESTIONS TO DISCUSS

1. Why is God's new race of grace characterized by being a living temple? What might being a living temple with your siblings in Christ look like in your life this week?

2. How does Paul's letter to Ephesus teach the first Christians about the bigness of Jesus' grace and our place in the family God? How can you share these truths with others?

3. Jesus created in himself one new people from Jews and Gentiles. The Greek term for "new" (*kainos*) means "new in kind." What does it mean for us to be a "new" kind of people? What implications does this have for the conversation about healing our racial divide?

GOSPEL BEHAVIORS TO PRACTICE

Write a letter explaining how Jesus' grace creates a new race and why this is important to God and for his church. Then share it with friends or on social media.

CHAPTER 11

AFFIRM THE RECONCILER'S CREED

I met Dr. John Perkins, or "JP," as he is affectionately called, when I was a seminary student in the early 2000s. I will never forget the imprint he left on me. I looked in awe at this man, who at the time was about sixty-eight. He was preaching with gospel fire accompanied by penetrating insights into the human condition with wisdom that only comes from living what you are proclaiming. Eloquence, knowledge, and truth erupted from him. The presence of the Holy Spirit was tangible. God's message was burning in his bones, and the flames of Jesus' grace raced through him to set us all on fire. But above all, he preached about King Jesus and the beautiful, reconciling power of the gospel. I did not know it at the time, but I was in the presence of a giant. I also did not know that JP's witness on reconciliation was so hard-won.

JP was born on a plantation, where enslaved Black people had picked cotton, in New Hebron, Mississippi. He was born during the Great Depression, so money and food were scarce. His mother died from malnutrition when he was a child. Let that sink in: his mother died *because there was not enough food to eat.* His grandmother took him in, and by third grade, JP stopped going to school because he was needed to work on the cotton farm.

Growing up in Mississippi, JP was always aware of the racism and the racial injustice Black people experienced. But in 1947, when his older brother Clyde, a World War II hero who had earned a Purple Heart, was killed by a New Hebron police officer, it became a matter of life and death. A White police officer had targeted Clyde at the movie theater, striking him in the back of the head with a club. Clyde, not knowing who had hit him, responded to the coward's attack with a defensive posture. When he did, the police officer fired two shots into his abdomen. JP was with his brother—an American hero—in the ambulance and in the Colored hospital when he died. JP's brother went all the way to Europe to fight against Hitler and the Nazis only to die at the hands of a racist police officer in America.

After his brother was murdered by the police officer, JP moved to California to escape the racism of Mississippi. He resolved to never move back.

In 1949, JP met the love of his life and future ministry

partner, Vera Mae Buckley. JP was drafted into the Korean War in 1951, and he and Vera Mae were married after basic training.

At the age of twenty-seven, while he and his family lived in California, JP started attending a Good News Club. He asked his son, Spencer, what he was learning at church, and Spencer told him that Jesus loves all the people of the world: the Black, the White, the Brown, and the Yellow. Jesus died to forgive the sins of all people and put them in his family. His son's simple words opened JP's eyes to the love of God. JP met Jesus.

JP and his family went back to Mississippi in 1960 to make a difference for the cause of Christ. He believed the gospel of Jesus Christ, civil rights, and economic development for the poor and oppressed were not enemies but allies.

JP was arrested in 1970 while visiting nineteen Tougaloo College students who had been put in jail after a peaceful protest march. Being a son of Mississippi, he was aware of the deep-seated racism and police brutality that were used to oppress and intimidate Black people. But he was not ready for the torture he endured at the hate-driven hands of the sheriff and the Mississippi Highway Patrol in Brandon, Mississippi. They repeatedly kicked him in his groin. They shoved a fork up his nose. They took a steel ball and smashed his hands over and over. He felt like he was dying, but somehow he was still alive. And after they had beaten him, he was forced to clean up his own blood.[1]

Tears streamed down JP's face as he recounted the story

years later. In a conversation over dinner, he told me, "Pastor, when those White police officers were terrorizing me, I saw them as less than human. I saw them as maggots. If I'd had a nuclear grenade, I would have detonated it and killed them and me. They filled me with hate." But he told me, "Then I realized I was a bigot too. But I knew as a Christian, I cannot hate these men. I must love. I want to preach a gospel strong enough to heal this madness and hatred."[2] JP writes,

> For too long, many in the Church have argued that unity in the body of Christ across ethnic and class lines is a separate issue from the gospel. There has been the suggestion that we can be reconciled to God without being reconciled to our brothers and sisters in Christ. Scripture doesn't bear that out. . . . It's going to take intentionally multiethnic and multicultural churches to bust through the chaos and confusion of the present moment and redirect our gaze to the revolutionary gospel of reconciliation.[3]

For more than six decades, JP—the Black man from rural Mississippi with only a third-grade education—has changed the world. He has been awarded numerous honorary doctorates for living out biblical reconciliation and justice.

JP is a modern-day apostle Paul, a giant in our midst, demonstrating the gospel of reconciliation and equipping us to do likewise. He has prophetically called Christians to be who Jesus declares us to be—ambassadors gifted with the ministry of reconciliation. He wants us to fulfill the privilege and responsibility that God has given us. This is every believer's calling:

> Everything is from God, who has reconciled us
> to himself through Christ and has given us the
> ministry of reconciliation. That is, in Christ, God
> was reconciling the world to himself, not counting
> their trespasses against them, and he has committed
> the message of reconciliation to us. Therefore, we
> are ambassadors for Christ, since God is making his
> appeal through us. We plead on Christ's behalf, "Be
> reconciled to God."
>
> 2 CORINTHIANS 5:18-20

As we conclude our look at what it means to follow Jesus in color-blessed discipleship, I want to provide you with a tool I've developed that will equip you to walk the often difficult road of reconciliation: the Reconciler's Creed.

The Reconciler's Creed

One of the "Derwinisms" that the congregation at Transformation Church often hears is "The scene of the crime is your mind." What I mean by this is that how we think influences how we live. We must partner with the Holy Spirit in allowing Christ to form, renew, and shape how we think. Dark powers want to influence our thinking; therefore, we must intentionally set our minds above, where Christ is seated, allowing him to transform our minds as we soak in the sacred Scriptures.[4]

The apostle Paul writes, "The weapons we fight with are not the weapons of the world. On the contrary, they have divine power to demolish strongholds. We demolish arguments and every pretension that sets itself up against the knowledge of God, and we take captive every thought to make it obedient to Christ" (2 Corinthians 10:4-5, NIV). "Tak[ing] captive every thought" empowers us to develop the mind of Christ. The mind of Christ guides us in navigating this broken planet as ambassadors of reconciliation. Taking every thought captive is a holy habit that increases our gospel effectiveness.

As Ralph Waldo Emerson reportedly said, "Sow a thought and you reap an action; sow an act and you reap a habit; sow a habit and you reap a character; sow a character and you reap a destiny."

I've developed the Reconciler's Creed so that we can fill our minds with and be formed by the gospel. A creed is a statement of theological beliefs designed to help you live out what you believe. Throughout church history, creeds have been written down to codify truths and solidify the church's beliefs on certain matters. They are often recited as a testimony and as an act of unity.

What follows are the five points of the Reconciler's Creed. After this short creed, you'll find an explanation of each of these five points to help you better understand and live its truths. At the end of this chapter, you'll also find the "Declaration of Reconciliation," which flows from this creed.

Consider reciting and discussing this creed weekly, preferably with your family, friends, and church community. Then live it.

1. **Worship:** We will relentlessly worship God by loving our brothers and sisters of different ethnicities in Christ (Matthew 22:37-40). According to Jesus, loving God and loving others are the greatest commandments, and they go together.

2. **Justification:** We will relentlessly see our brothers and sisters of other ethnicities as the righteousness of God in Christ (Romans 3:22). We are all covered in the same justifying blood.

3. **Holiness:** We will relentlessly ask God the Holy Spirit to purge us of any prejudices that we have in our hearts (Romans 8:28-29; Galatians 4:19). Honest self-examination is vital to healing and maturity.

4. **Unity:** We will relentlessly pursue and live in the unity Jesus secured through the bloody cross (Ephesians 2:14-16). We do not work for unity; we live from unity in Christ.

5. **Guard:** We will relentlessly guard our unity in Christ (Ephesians 4:1-6). Our unity in Christ is a gift and treasure that must be guarded. Demonic powers and those under the power of the evil one want to divide God's people. Our unity displays the beauty of our risen Redeemer; our disunity is a poor witness.

The Reconciler's Creed helps us to live Holy Spirit–empowered, cross-shaped lives of vertical and horizontal reconciliation.

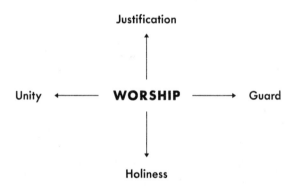

Here's a more thorough explanation of the Reconciler's Creed.

Worship

What comes to mind when you hear the word *worship*? I suspect our minds are filled with beautifully arranged music, played with exquisite skill, exalting Christ. A vital aspect of worship is singing songs of praise and worship. Worship tells us who God is, and praise reminds us of what God has done. Our Father in heaven loves to hear his children singing to him.[5] Paul encouraged the multiethnic church in Ephesus that was wrestling with unity,

> Don't act thoughtlessly, but understand what the
> Lord wants you to do. Don't be drunk with wine,
> because that will ruin your life. Instead, be filled
> with the Holy Spirit, singing psalms and hymns
> and spiritual songs among yourselves, and making
> music to the Lord in your hearts. And give thanks
> for everything to God the Father in the name of
> our Lord Jesus Christ.
>
> EPHESIANS 5:17-20, NLT

Our singing is a means by which we remember the acts of God in Christ and remember who our Father is. But the greatest worship song we can sing is a life of loving God totally (upward), ourselves rightly (inward), and our neighbors mercifully (outward).[6] In response to the Father's mercy in Jesus, we love him by becoming living sacrifices,[7]

> having the same love, united in spirit, intent on
> one purpose. Do nothing out of selfish ambition
> or conceit, but in humility consider others as more
> important than yourselves. Everyone should look

not to his own interests, but rather to the interests
of others. Adopt the same attitude as that of Christ
Jesus.

PHILIPPIANS 2:2-5

Worship is recognizing and honoring the image of God
in your fellow human being. One of the grace gifts the Spirit
gives to Abba's kids is the ability to see human beings as
God sees them, "remarkably and wondrously made" (Psalm
139:14). Love is not apathetic to the plight of brothers and
sisters of different ethnicities suffering under the boot of
injustice and prejudice. Because "there is no Jew or Greek,
slave or free, male and female, since you are all one in Christ
Jesus" (Galatians 3:28), our love in Christ Jesus compels us
to cross the color line, break down the class divide, and blow
up the barriers of sexism.

Worship is relentlessly loving your brothers and sisters
of different ethnicities, seeing the beauty of their color and
culture. James, the half brother of Jesus and leader of the first
Christians, wrote, "Yes indeed, it is good when you obey the
royal law as found in the Scriptures: 'Love your neighbor
as yourself.' But if you favor some people over others, you
are committing a sin. You are guilty of breaking the law"
(James 2:8-9, NLT). Worship is what we were made to do,
and in doing what we were made to do, Jesus is glorified in
his people and through his people. We become a sign and
foretaste of the new heaven and new earth:

After this I looked, and there was a vast multitude
from every nation, tribe, people, and language,
which no one could number, standing before the
throne and before the Lamb. They were clothed
in white robes with palm branches in their hands.
And they cried out in a loud voice:

> Salvation belongs to our God,
> who is seated on the throne,
> and to the Lamb!

REVELATION 7:9-10

Justification

When I met Jesus in 1997, I was mesmerized by his love,
undone by his grace, and wrecked by his mercy. I distinctly
remember being in the kitchen of our home in Indianapolis,
talking to Vicki about Galatians 2:20: "I have been crucified
with Christ, and I no longer live, but Christ lives in me. The
life I now live in the body, I live by faith in the Son of God,
who loved me and gave himself for me."

As I read that text, it became clear that King Jesus provides us with the love we were created for and the value we
crave. I was blown away that he gave himself for us. What
in the world could we ever achieve that could eclipse the
Son of God giving himself for us? The value of something
is determined by what it costs. Jesus paid the ultimate price
for us; therefore, every child of God is valuable. The apostle

Peter writes, "You know that you were redeemed from your empty way of life inherited from your ancestors, not with perishable things like silver or gold, but with the precious blood of Christ, like that of an unblemished and spotless lamb" (1 Peter 1:18-19).

Jesus provides the *love* we need, the *value* we want, and the *power* we lack to live the life he calls us to. How unfathomable it is that Jesus himself indwells all of his people! Jesus gave his life *for* us to live his life *in* us and *through* us. What is our part? Faith. We must trust God that what he has promised is true and must live our lives from his faithfulness.

As a football player, trusting my coaches, teammates, and playbook was an act of faith essential to my and my team's success. During my sophomore year at Brigham Young University in 1990, I made my first career start versus the University of New Mexico. It was my big chance. I knew for me to be successful and help my team, I had to study my playbook, practice with intentionality and intensity, and watch lots of my opponents' game film so I could be ready. As a result of my preparation, I intercepted three passes and scored a touchdown. I set a stadium record that still exists today—more than thirty years later! I helped my team win because I trusted my coaches, their defensive game plan, my teammates, and my preparation.

Walking by faith is similar. It means we trust our coaches (God, Jesus, the Holy Spirit), teammates (other mature Christians), and playbook (Scripture) as we live our lives. The apostle Paul gives us another window into what it means:

Since you have been raised to new life with Christ,
set your sights on the realities of heaven, where
Christ sits in the place of honor at God's right hand.
Think about the things of heaven, not the things of
earth. For you died to this life, and *your real life is
hidden with Christ in God.*

COLOSSIANS 3:1-3, NLT, EMPHASIS ADDED

As the multiethnic, redeemed family of God, we must see
not only *ourselves* as being in Christ; we must see *each other*
as being in Christ. The moment we said yes to Jesus, an epic
exchange took place. All that is true about Jesus became true
about us. We are eternally united to him.

But that's just it: it's not only *you* who has experienced
this reality. If God has united *you* to Jesus, then he has also
done a great thing for your brothers and sisters of different
ethnicities. Regardless of our ethnicity, we are equally blessed
because we are equally united to Christ,[8] and we should treat
each other that way. This act of justification overwhelms me:

The law, then, was our guardian until Christ, so that
we could be justified by faith. But since that faith
has come, we are no longer under a guardian, for
through faith you are all sons of God in Christ Jesus.
For those of you who were baptized into Christ have
been clothed with Christ. There is no Jew or Greek,
slave or free, male and female; since you are all one in

Christ Jesus. And if you belong to Christ, then you are
Abraham's seed, heirs according to the promise.

GALATIANS 3:24-29

Justification is the loving act of the Father, the Son, and
the Holy Spirit uniting and incorporating believers into the
righteousness of Jesus. His faithfulness to God, in perfect
obedience, in all the ways we could not obey on our own,
is given to us as a gift.[9] Every child of God is forgiven,
reconciled, acceptable, and pleasing to the Father because
they are clothed in Jesus' righteousness. God's family is
equally righteous in Christ. It was the doctrine of justification that Paul taught to rid his first-century churches of
Gentile supremacy and Jewish supremacy. The doctrine of
justification declares the supremacy of Jesus because we all
need his righteousness.

When I first met Jesus, I was so in love with him for making *me* righteous. But then I sensed the Holy Spirit saying,
"Now it is time to see and treat your brothers and sisters
as the righteousness of the Messiah." It changed everything.
First, it intensified my love for Jesus and the greatness of salvation. I finally saw hope for God's people to be the means
of healing the racial divide. Second, my wife and I decided
that we would plant a gospel-shaped, multiethnic church
that would reach the lost and cultivate a congregation of disciples that are color-blessed, not colorblind. We would be a
community of missionaries, reconcilers, and justice seekers.
Third, any form of prejudice was no longer welcome in my

heart. I was now going to be known as an extremist of love. Because when we see one another as the righteousness of Christ—loved and accepted in the Father's sight and empowered by the Holy Spirit—there is no room for superiority or contempt, but only love.

Holiness

One of the most beautiful, audacious, and glorious descriptions of God and how his multicolored family are to relate to him, each other, and the world was uttered by the apostle Peter, quoting Leviticus: "For it is written, Be holy, because I am holy" (1 Peter 1:16).

But what is the holiness of God? A. W. Tozer writes this of God's holiness:

> He is the absolute quintessence of moral excellence, infinitely perfect in righteousness, purity, rectitude, and incomprehensible holiness. And in all this He is uncreated, self-sufficient and beyond the power of human thought to conceive or human speech to utter. . . . Holy is the way God is. To be holy He does not conform to a standard. He is the standard. He is absolutely holy with an infinite, incomprehensible fullness of purity that is incapable of being other than it is. Because He is holy, His attributes are holy; that is, whatever we think of as belonging to God must be thought of as holy.[10]

God—that is, the Father, the Son, and the Spirit—is utterly *hágios* (set apart). He is unique in his tripersonal being and is beyond comparison at every level of his being. Yet in Messiah Jesus, in an act of grace that transcends measurement, through a kindness, compassion, and mercy that is epic, all who trust Jesus as their King are "forever made perfect" (Hebrews 10:14, NLT). And "God has united you with Christ Jesus. For our benefit God made him to be wisdom itself. Christ made us right with God; he made us pure and holy, and he freed us from sin" (1 Corinthians 1:30, NLT). The interethnic family that God promised Abraham is holy because the living, holy God of love incorporated us in his Son, Jesus. Holiness is not something we can achieve; it is a gift we *receive*. It is the power to live as we were intended to live.

Therefore, how can a child of God look down on another brother or sister in Christ if we all share equally in his holiness?

How can a child of God, whose worth is found in Jesus alone, be hateful toward a brother or sister of a different ethnicity or economic class, if we belong to a holy God?

How can children of God sit silently as their brothers and sisters experience racial injustice?

When the Son rises in our souls, pushing back the darkness of night, we are awakened to love people with the holy love with which God in Christ loved us. This is holiness. This is the good life.[11]

Like today, in the first century, the apostle Paul had the monumental task of equipping and shepherding the multiethnic, multiclass churches in Colossae to live out in community the holiness God gave them as a gift of grace. These churches were experiencing conflict—I am sure they disagreed politically and socially too. They were lying about each other, slandering each other, not forgiving each other, and acting with malicious anger toward each other.[12] These behaviors are beneath the people of God. They bear witness to demonic powers, not the risen King.

So how does Paul move them from unholiness to holiness?

First, he tells them to set their minds on Jesus. He encourages the Jews, the Gentiles, the rich, the poor, the men, and the women to set their minds on Jesus and to remember to "put on your new nature, and be renewed as you learn to know your Creator and become like him. In this new life, it doesn't matter if you are a Jew or a Gentile, circumcised or uncircumcised, barbaric, uncivilized, slave, or free. Christ is all that matters, and he lives in all of us" (Colossians 3:10-11, NLT).

Second, Paul reminds them of their new identity as God's chosen ones. He says, "God chose you to be the holy people he loves" (Colossians 3:12, NLT). All who trust in Jesus are God's elect, or chosen ones, in Christ.[13] Just as the Father adores and treasures Jesus, he adores and treasures all of us who reside in Christ. We are united and incorporated into Jesus, God's chosen one.[14]

Third, he calls them to obedience. He writes,

Clothe yourselves with tenderhearted mercy, kindness, humility, gentleness, and patience. Make allowance

for each other's faults, and forgive anyone who offends
you. Remember, the Lord forgave you, so you must
forgive others. Above all, clothe yourselves with love,
which binds us all together in perfect harmony. And
let the peace that comes from Christ rule in your
hearts. For as members of one body you are called to
live in peace. And always be thankful.

COLOSSIANS 3:12-15, NLT

Dream with me for a moment. What if all of God's beautifully diverse family members acted in faith and treated each
other this way as the presence of God, through the Spirit,
guided us and empowered us to be Jesus to each other?

Can you imagine how different the church would be?
God's people are to be salt and light, a means of grace to a
world deeply divided. Our unity in Christ, fueled by holy
living, becomes a lighthouse in an ocean of chaos.

Think about this: Israel was given the vocation of helping
the Gentiles get free from idolatry. But Israel itself was lost in
idolatry. The church has the vocation of helping the world
to be free of the dark powers that create sins like racism and
division. But like Israel, the church is often as deeply divided
as our culture.

God is calling a holy people to break the powers of darkness and to be who we were meant to be:

But you are not like that, for you are a chosen
people. You are royal priests, a holy nation, God's

very own possession. As a result, you can show others the goodness of God, for he called you out of the darkness into his wonderful light.

1 PETER 2:9, NLT

As God's people, we must relentlessly ask God the Holy Spirit to purge us of any prejudices in our hearts. Honest self-examination is vital to healing and maturity.

Unity

We've looked in other chapters at how the individualistic gospel of the United States is a perversion of discipleship. The antidote—the vision of discipleship that the Bible gives us—is wholistic, communal, and unified in Christ.

Unity mattered to Jesus:

I pray that they will all be one, just as you and I are one—as you are in me, Father, and I am in you. And may they be in us so that the world will believe you sent me.

JOHN 17:21, NLT

Unity mattered to the apostle Paul:

Therefore I, the prisoner in the Lord, urge you to walk worthy of the calling you have received, with all humility and gentleness, with patience, bearing with

one another in love, making every effort to keep the
unity of the Spirit through the bond of peace.

EPHESIANS 4:1-3

The Greek word for "unity" is *henótēs*, meaning a state of
oneness. For those adopted into God's family through faith
in the risen Christ, we are now a unified family, consist-
ing of all the ethnicities of the earth. This gospel reality is
so hard for us to grasp because we are soaked in Western
individualism.

Historically, "each phase of Western Philosophy has put
forth as its central tenet the primacy of the individual."[15]
The church in America has transformed the gospel from a
corporate, communal understanding to an individualistic,
privatized faith. The gospel becomes a story of how Jesus
came to save *me* from the wrath of God, to help *me* with life's
problems, and to help *me* reach heaven when I die. In reality,
the gospel is a story of God through the Messiah rescuing,
reconciling, and redeeming a people from *all* ethnicities, who
exist for *his* glory, embody *his* justice, and fulfill *his* mission
as a foretaste of *his* Kingdom.

Jesus redeems us individually so our faith can be expressed
communally and socially. When we privatize our faith, we
lose our social conscience, neglecting issues of justice that do
not affect us or only affect people that are not in our same
ethnic or socioeconomic group. In Christ, we are brothers
and sisters; thus, we are our brothers' (and sisters') keepers.
Your problem is my problem because we are the body of

Christ. All justice is social. Paul writes, "Just as our bodies have many parts and each part has a special function, so it is with Christ's body. We are many parts of one body, and we all belong to each other" (Romans 12:5, NLT).

Unity within diversity makes sense when we realize that God himself is unity within diversity.[16] "God"—that is, the Father, the Son, and the Holy Spirit—"is love" (1 John 4:8). God is eternal existence—no beginning, no end. Forever and always, the Father, the Son, and the Holy Spirit have loved each other.

Love requires community. A solitary being cannot be loving because there is no one else to love. God, who is a community of love, invites humanity to share in his everlasting love through the gift of eternal life.

We experience unity in diversity in our salvation: God the Father chose us in Christ. God the Son redeems us through his blood. God the Holy Spirit seals, fills, and indwells us.[17]

When we are baptized, we are baptized in the name (singular) of the Father, the Son, and the Holy Spirit (plural): "Go, therefore, and make disciples of all nations [*ethnos*], baptizing them in the name of the Father and of the Son and of the Holy Spirit" (Matthew 28:19).

Even in our missional call, we are to make disciples—that is, followers of Jesus—from all ethnicities. We are baptized into Christ and equally share in his life. The idea of ethnic pride or prejudice is offensive to God and his great salvation. God has eternally loved diversity. Humanity's ethnic diversity reflects the triune God's image and likeness.

Because unity matters to God, it is a spiritual discipline that we must practice and participate in as children of the Father. Learning to love our brothers and sisters is a gift that makes us more human, as those who are different from us show us different aspects of being redeemed in Christ.

Unity does not mean uniformity. Jesus redeems our ethnic and cultural differences so that we can enhance one another. The wondrous array of the diversity that exists throughout the ethnicities and cultures of humanity echoes the unity and diversity of God. The Father loves for his children to be unified in his Son through the Holy Spirit. Look at how grand and beautiful this picture of our future is. How could we not fight racism and racial injustice considering our epic future?

And they sang a new song:

> You are worthy to take the scroll
> and to open its seals,
> because you were slaughtered,
> and you purchased people
> for God by your blood
> from every tribe and language
> and people and nation.
> You made them a kingdom
> and priests to our God,
> and they will reign on the earth.
>
> REVELATION 5:9-10

Dark powers love to divide. Jesus loves to unite.

Sin separates. Jesus regenerates.

Dark powers exclude. Jesus includes.

The nanosecond you said yes to Jesus, regardless of your ethnicity or social status, you were eternally united to him. All that is true of Jesus is now true of you forever. Your identity is now tied to Jesus. And he will not let go of the rope. This is true because of his life, his atoning death on the cross, and his resurrection.[18]

Inclusion into the family that God promised Abraham cannot be achieved. It can only be received by faith.[19] By faith, God the Holy Spirit incorporates us into Jesus. Not only are *you* incorporated, but so is every other person who calls on his name. The body of Christ is the place where all of God's children are located: "Now you are the body of Christ, and individual members of it" (1 Corinthians 12:27).

You are united to brothers and sisters of different ethnicities, socioeconomic classes, and political parties. In Christ, this is true. You do not choose who your brothers and sisters are; God does. And he calls us to love each other with the love Christ loved us with.[20]

Guard

In 1993, I was the fourth-round draft pick of the Indianapolis Colts. I thought I was a big deal . . . until I got to training camp. During practice one day, I commented to my defensive back teammates that I did not think one of the other veteran defensive backs knew what he was doing out on the field. Later in practice, another veteran defensive back who had heard my comment told that player what I'd said. He straight up called me out because what I said to the other defensive backs was divisive. I should have taken my concern directly to the veteran player instead of talking about him disrespectfully to the other defensive backs. I was not guarding the unity of the team; I was creating disunity. A disunified team is a losing team.

The veteran player looked at me seriously and said, "If you have concerns about me not knowing what I am doing on the field, let's talk about it and work it out. In a few weeks, we are going to be playing real games. We must be on the same page."

The veteran players taught me a lesson I needed to learn: guard the unity of the team. Do not spread division. Be a unifier; be a team builder.

As blood-bought children of the living God, we are the body of Christ, belonging to one another. Paul writes, "Therefore I, the prisoner in the Lord, urge you to walk worthy of the calling you have received, with all humility and gentleness, with patience, bearing with one another in love, making every effort to keep the unity of the Spirit through the bond of peace" (Ephesians 4:1-3).

The Greek word for "keep" (*tēréō*) literally means "to guard." Every single follower of Jesus is a guardian. We are not Guardians of the Galaxy; we are guardians of the unity that Jesus created through his death on the cross. Your brothers

AFFIRM THE RECONCILER'S CREED

and sisters—regardless of ethnicity, socioeconomic class, or gender—are called to guard the unity we have in Christ. Jesus is the bond that draws us into his circle of peace. We do not live to create unity and peace. We live *from* the unity and peace Jesus already created. Therefore, we can have honest conversations when we see other members of the body act in ways that cause division.

As we saw in chapter 5, the apostle Paul, a Jewish man, confronted another Jewish man, Peter, when Peter created disunity in the multiethnic church at Antioch when he stopped eating with the Gentiles because "he feared those from the circumcision party" (Galatians 2:12). Peter's hypocrisy caused the other Jews to do the same. One racist act caused other good men to act in an ungodly way and separate from the Gentiles. The apostle Paul loved Jesus and his church; therefore, he opposed Peter to his face. This is what love does. Love corrects brothers and sisters when they are creating disunity. It is vital that we have gospel courage to care enough about the redemptive, unifying work that Jesus bled to purchase that we are willing to guard the unity within the body of Christ. Our unity in Christ is a treasure that deserves being guarded. Our unity displays the beauty of our risen Redeemer.

The Declaration of Reconciliation

Now that you have read and understand the Reconciler's Creed, I hope you will join me in praying the Declaration of Reconciliation:

THE DECLARATION OF RECONCILIATION

God of Abraham, Isaac, and Jacob,
Blessed King of the universe,
in your eternal Son, Messiah Jesus,
the King of kings,
the one who is grace upon grace and
who created a new race, made of all of the human race,
through his life, death, and resurrection—
in his name, by the Holy Spirit's power,
we offer ourselves as living sacrifices, dwelling places of God.
King Jesus, we affirm that you purchased a richly diverse
    people for your Father,
a people declared righteous by your blood,
a people who are one, yet many.
Your blood binds us to you and to each other as
    a beautiful mosaic.
We worship you by loving one another.
We are the family of the redeemed.
We belong to the King.
We pledge our allegiance to King Jesus, the Lamb of God
    who sits on the throne.
May we live from and guard the unity Jesus secured on
    the cross.
As we grow in holiness, Spirit, empower us to reflect Jesus
    more and more.
May the world see we love Jesus by the way we love each
    other.
May we treasure our brothers and sisters more than we

treasure economic interests, political affiliations, fears,
or cultural customs.
In your name, King Jesus,
we pray,
Amen.

Again, this is the charge that is given to every believer:

Everything is from God, who has reconciled us
to himself through Christ and has given us the
ministry of reconciliation. That is, in Christ, God
was reconciling the world to himself, not counting
their trespasses against them, and he has committed
the message of reconciliation to us. Therefore, we
are ambassadors for Christ, since God is making his
appeal through us. We plead on Christ's behalf, "Be
reconciled to God."

2 CORINTHIANS 5:18-20

May we be ambassadors for Christ, pleading with all
people, "Be reconciled to God."

| | | | **MARINATE ON THIS** | | | |

PRAYER

Father,
We are chosen in your eternal Son.
What is true of him is now true of us.
All your daughters and sons are clothed in righteousness
through your Son, Jesus.
In him, we are holy and loved without limit.
By the Holy Spirit's power,
we put on compassion, kindness, patience, gentleness,
humility, and, above all, love.
May we walk in unity, displaying the beauty of your gospel.
In Jesus' name,
Amen.

THINGS TO THINK ABOUT

- The Reconciler's Creed helps us to live Holy Spirit–empowered, cross-shaped lives of vertical and horizontal reconciliation.

- God's people are to be salt and light, a means of grace to a world deeply divided. Our unity in Christ, fueled by holy living, becomes a lighthouse in an ocean of chaos.

- Jesus redeems us individually so our faith can be expressed communally and socially. When we privatize our faith, we lose our social conscience, neglecting issues of justice that do not affect us or only affect people that are not in our same ethnic or socioeconomic group. In Christ, we are brothers and sisters; thus, we are our brothers' (and sisters') keepers.

- Unity does not mean uniformity. Jesus redeems our ethnic and cultural differences so that we can enhance one another. The wondrous array of the diversity that exists throughout the ethnicities and cultures of humanity echoes the unity and diversity of God.

QUESTIONS TO DISCUSS

1. Why is the ministry of reconciliation the call of every believer? What will it look like for you to participate in this ministry?

2. Consider the five points of the Reconciler's Creed: worship, justification, holiness, unity, and guard. Which one of these points resonates most with you? Why? Which of these beliefs do you think you are especially good at living? Which need work?

3. Unity mattered to Jesus and Paul and is a theme of the New Testament. Imagine for a few minutes what ethnic unity in your church context could look like this week, this month, this year, and five years from now. Describe what you've imagined. What next steps could you take to make what you've imagined a reality?

GOSPEL BEHAVIORS TO PRACTICE

Print copies of the Reconciler's Creed and the Declaration of Reconciliation and place them where you will see them regularly—around your house, in your office, in your car, in your Bible. Remember the truths included in them, and say them aloud—by yourself and with others—as you are able throughout the week.

PASSING THE TORCH

One Sunday a few years ago, I had just finished preaching and was greeting people and giving fist bumps when I noticed a thirtysomething White guy running toward me from the back of the room. *Is he running to attack me?* I wondered. I was not sure, but I needed to be ready just in case. As he got closer, I saw snot swinging from his nostrils and tears pouring down his face. Before I knew it, he was hugging me. I suspect the dangling snot ended up on my clothes.

He said, "I can't believe I'm in church. I can't believe you're Black. I do not even like Black people. But I want Jesus."

Once he calmed down a little, I said, "Tell me your story, man."

"My girlfriend has been asking me to come to church," he began. "I told her I will never go to a church with a Black preacher. I came today only to get her off my back. Besides, I cannot argue with how her life is transforming. I wanted to hate you, but as you preached, I couldn't stop listening. You kept talking about Jesus, and something happened in my heart. I want to be forgiven. I want him. I want to change."

Before this incredible moment of transformation, this man and his girlfriend had been on a journey. After serving several years in prison for drug charges, his girlfriend, Amber, had visited Transformation Church at the invitation of a friend. During a service, she met Jesus, and her life was forever changed. Eventually, she wanted her boyfriend, who also struggled with substance addiction, to embrace Jesus too. It took almost a year before he came with her and had his life transformed by Jesus.

After this emotional greeting, the couple was baptized and plugged into our community. They asked me if I would officiate their wedding, which I was excited to do. Amber stunned me by asking if I would walk her down the aisle and give her away. She asked me because her dad had disowned her at sixteen. Enthusiastically, I said, "Yes!"

The big day arrived. The bride wore blue jeans, cowboy boots, and a white short-sleeve button-down shirt that showed the barbed-wire tattoo around her left bicep. The groom wore a suit. Only a few people came, but the vibe was beautiful. The groom and I began the service at the pulpit.

When the processional started, I left him and ran to walk Amber down the aisle. She looked me in the eye and smiled.

I placed her hand in his. I walked behind the pulpit and asked, "Who gives this woman away?" Then I ran back around and said, "I do." And with that, the wedding proceeded normally. A Black pastor in South Carolina officiated the wedding of an ex-con White girl to a snotty-nosed former racist who had been transformed by Jesus.

This story that God graciously allowed me to participate in is the power of the gospel on display. This is the gospel I believe, and the gospel Paul believed and preached. Paul preached the beautiful mystery of Christ, which is that "the Gentiles are coheirs, members of the same body, and partners in the promise in Christ Jesus through the gospel" (Ephesians 3:6). He and the first Christians understood the bigness of the gospel. If the gospel is only about forgiving sins, then that gospel is too small. When our saving King lived a sinless life for us, died on the cross instead of us, and rose from the dead to live through us, he fulfilled his Father's promise to Abraham, creating a forgiven, redeemed, reconciled, multicolored, multiethnic family. All who call on the name of Jesus—Black, White, Asian, Latino, Jewish, and Indigenous—are included in this long-promised family.

As I write, the 2020 Summer Olympic Games are soon to begin (a year later than planned). There's something about the Summer Olympic Games that inspires me. I remember as a little boy watching Carl Lewis sprinting and long jumping his way to multiple gold medals. And who could forget the

Dream Team with Michael Jordan, Magic Johnson, Larry Bird, and so many other NBA greats? What about Simone Biles, the greatest gymnast the world has ever witnessed, and the unmatched Michael Phelps, who swam with the speed and power of a marine animal? Then there is the iconic Jesse Owens, who dominated Nazi Germany in the 1936 Summer Games in Berlin. But I think I am inspired most by the torch relay. The torch relay "celebrates the passing of the sacred flame from one torch to the next."[1]

In reading this book, you've seen how the Bible is the epic story of God fulfilling his promise to Abraham through the work of Jesus Christ. You've seen how the earliest followers of Jesus, rather than splitting into separate Jewish and Gentile congregations, were called "Christians" because they represented a new, unified people under the Christ (Messiah). And you've also hopefully caught the vision of what following Jesus in color-blessed discipleship might look like in your life and in the lives of your church and community.

Today, I am passing the sacred flame of gospel reconciliation to you. God the Holy Spirit, as he did in the first Christians, wants to set your heart ablaze with his power and his passion to see people love God and each other through Christ Jesus.

There is no better time than now to be a healer and reconciler. There is too much at stake for us to be indifferent or complacent. Reconciliation matters to God; therefore, it must matter to us. For such a time as this, God has brought this book into your life. Take this message, live it, spread it, share it, and train others to do the same. Take the flame. It's yours now. Let's be the generation that says, "Enough is enough. We are going to heal the racial divide. This is our divine birthright as sons and daughters of God." Our God is great. His gospel is great. He has given us a great calling. May we answer the call with "Here I am; send me."

Pass the flame.

Is there any encouragement from belonging to Christ? Any comfort from his love? Any fellowship together in the Spirit? Are your hearts tender and compassionate? Then make me truly happy by agreeing wholeheartedly with each other, loving one another, and working together with one mind and purpose. Don't be selfish; don't try to impress others. Be humble, thinking of others as better than yourselves. Don't look out only for your own interests, but take an interest in others, too.

PHILIPPIANS 2:1-4, NLT

Acknowledgments

I'm grateful to so many people who have made this book possible.

Alexander, thanks for being a great agent. Jon Farrar and Jan Long Harris of Tyndale, thanks for enthusiastically believing in me and this book. Chris McGinn, thanks for editing another one of my books—you are awesome. Jonathan Schindler, thank you for taking my manuscript and making it so much better! The editing process with you was such an encouragement.

Alex and Kristel, I'm so thankful you are on my team. Your passion, skills, and insights are invaluable.

Transformation Church, for twelve years, by God's grace, you have lived so much of this book. What I write about is possible because I have seen it in you.

Vicki, my queen, my best friend, and my ministry partner, thank you for your strength and love. We have been teammates since 1990. Presley, my daughter and firstborn, your resilience and love keep me going. And your laugh. I love to hear your laugh. Jeremiah, my son, your love and friendship are a gift to me. Thank you. And Connie Gray, my momma, thank you for having me when you were only seventeen. And thanks for listening to the Billy Graham sermons when I was in your tummy!

And last but not least, King Jesus, thank you for loving me, saving me, transforming me, and living in me. I love you the most. Be pleased with the book.

Notes

INTRODUCTION: THE NEW NORMAL
1. See Genesis 12:1-3; Galatians 3:8.
2. N. T. Wright, *Galatians*, Commentaries for Christian Formation (Grand Rapids, MI: Eerdmans, 2021), 92.

CHAPTER 1: "WHY DO YOU TALK ABOUT RACE SO MUCH?"
1. See Ephesians 2:14-16; 3:5-11.
2. Rodney Stark, *The Rise of Christianity: How the Obscure, Marginal Jesus Movement Became the Dominant Religious Force in the Western World in a Few Centuries* (San Francisco: HarperSanFrancisco, 1997), 158.
3. See Exodus 1:15-21.
4. See Esther 3:5-6.
5. See Ephesians 3:6, 10-11. "The rulers and authorities" refers to the demonic realm.
6. Martin Luther King Jr., "Letter from a Birmingham Jail," April 16, 1963, African Studies Center, University of Pennsylvania, https://www.africa.upenn.edu/Articles_Gen/Letter_Birmingham.html.

CHAPTER 2: A FAMILY FOR ABRAHAM
1. Christopher J. H. Wright, *The Mission of God: Unlocking the Bible's Grand Narrative* (Downers Grove, IL: IVP Academic, 2013), 189, ebook.
2. Colossians 1:15, NLT.
3. Lisa Sharon Harper, *The Very Good Gospel: How Everything Wrong Can Be Made Right* (New York: WaterBrook, 2016), 140.
4. Jemar Tisby, *How to Fight Racism: Courageous Christianity and the Journey toward Racial Justice* (Grand Rapids, MI: Zondervan Reflective, 2021), 21.

5. J. Daniel Hays, *From Every People and Nation: A Biblical Theology of Race,* New Studies in Biblical Theology, vol. 14 (Downers Grove, IL: InterVarsity Press, 2003), 61.
6. See Galatians 3:8.
7. Wright, *Mission of God*, 193.
8. Wright, 193.
9. See Galatians 3:16.
10. See John 3:1-8.
11. N. T. Wright, *Galatians,* Commentaries for Christian Formation (Grand Rapids, MI: Eerdmans, 2021), 172–73.
12. See Ephesians 1:10-14.
13. See Philippians 2:12; Romans 8:28-29; Galatians 4:19.
14. Justo L. González, *For the Healing of the Nations: The Book of Revelation in an Age of Cultural Conflict* (Maryknoll, NY: Orbis Books, 2005), 92.
15. See Ephesians 3:6-11.
16. John D. Barry et al. eds., *Faithlife Study Bible* (Bellingham, WA: Lexham Press, 2016), Exodus 12:38 study note.
17. Hays, *From Every People and Nation,* 71.
18. Isaiah 42:6-8, NLT. See also 55:5.
19. See Matthew 1:2-6.
20. See Ephesians 2:1-22.
21. Wright, *Mission of God*, 193.
22. See Ephesians 1:10-14.

CHAPTER: 3 JESUS THE BARRIER BREAKER AND FAMILY MAKER

1. See Psalm 119:116, 174; Isaiah 52:10; 42:6, 9; 46:13.
2. See Joshua 2:13; 6:17, 23, 25; Hebrews 11:31.
3. See Genesis 38:12-24.
4. See 2 Samuel 11.
5. See Galatians 3:16.
6. N. T. Wright, *Luke for Everyone,* The New Testament for Everyone (Louisville, KY: Westminster John Knox, 2004), 48.
7. Bob Utley, *Luke the Historian: The Gospel of Luke* (Marshall, TX: Bible Lessons International, 2004), Luke 10:33.
8. Flavius Josephus, *The Works of Josephus: Complete and Unabridged,* trans. William Whiston (Peabody, MA: Hendrickson, 1987), 478.
9. Denise Kimber Buell, *Why This New Race: Ethnic Reasoning in Early Christianity* (New York: Columbia University Press, 2005), 4.
10. Craig S. Keener, *The IVP Bible Background Commentary: New Testament,* 2nd ed. (Downers Grove, IL: IVP Academic, 2014), 259.

11. See, for example, Mark 1:23-26, 34, 40-44; 8:27-30.
12. See John 4:35.
13. Utley, *Luke the Historian*, Luke 10:30.
14. John D. Barry et al. eds., *Faithlife Study Bible* (Bellingham, WA: Lexham Press, 2016), Luke 10:35 study note.
15. See 1 Kings 8:41-43.
16. See Isaiah 2:2-5; 19:19-25; 42:6; 49:6; 60:5.
17. Utley, *Luke the Historian*, Luke 19:45.
18. Utley, Luke 19:45.
19. Utley, Luke 19:45.
20. Curtiss Paul DeYoung et al., *United by Faith: The Multiracial Congregation as an Answer to the Problem of Race* (New York: Oxford University Press, 2003), 15.
21. DeYoung et al., 15.
22. William Barclay, *The Letters to the Galatians and Ephesians*, The New Daily Study Bible, rev. ed. (Louisville, KY: Westminster John Knox Press, 2002), 130.
23. Barclay, 130.
24. Barclay, 130.
25. Barclay, 130.
26. For the Jewish feeding, see Mark 6:34-44. For the Gentile Decapolis feeding, see Mark 8:1-10.

CHAPTER 4: THE BIRTH OF GOD'S MULTIETHNIC FAMILY

1. See Genesis 12:1-3; Galatians 3:8.
2. For more on the Feast of Weeks, see Exodus 34:22; Deuteronomy 16:10.
3. Bob Utley, *Luke the Historian: The Book of Acts* (Marshall, TX: Bible Lessons International, 2003), Acts 2:9.
4. See, for example, Deuteronomy 14:28-29; James 1:27.
5. Vince Bantu writes, "It is more likely that this eunuch was a representative of the court of Candace, the Cushite queen of Meroe." Vince L. Bantu, *A Multitude of All Peoples: Engaging Ancient Christianity's Global Identity*, Missiological Engagements (Downers Grove, IL: IVP Academic, 2020), 97.
6. Bantu, 118.
7. See Galatians 3:24-29.
8. I got this term from Dr. David Anderson. See David A. Anderson, *Gracism: The Art of Inclusion* (Downers Grove, IL: IVP Books, 2007).

CHAPTER 5: PAUL AND THE EARLY CHURCH

1. See Acts 9:1-5; Philippians 2:5-11; 1 Corinthians 5:7; Romans 3:21-26; 5:12; 8:28-29; 15:8-13; Hebrews 8:6; Ephesians 1:5-14; 2:14.
2. See Ephesians 3:4-11; 2:13-16.
3. See 2 Corinthians 5:18-20.
4. The information in this paragraph is from Scot McKnight, *A Fellowship of Differents: Showing the World God's Design for Life Together* (Grand Rapids, MI: Zondervan, 2015), 237.
5. See Acts 5:34-39.
6. Rodney Stark, *The Rise of Christianity: How the Obscure, Marginal Jesus Movement Became the Dominant Religious Force in the Western World in a Few Centuries* (San Francisco: HarperSanFrancisco, 1997), 157.
7. Stark, *Rise of Christianity*, 158.
8. Denise Kimber Buell, *Why This New Race: Ethnic Reasoning in Early Christianity* (New York: Columbia University Press, 2005), 2.
9. See Matthew 8:11.
10. See Galatians 6:15; Romans 2:25-29.
11. Derwin L. Gray, *Building a Multiethnic Church: A Gospel Vision of Love, Grace, and Reconciliation in a Divided World* (Nashville, TN: Thomas Nelson, 2021), 60.
12. Curtiss Paul DeYoung et al., *United by Faith: The Multiracial Congregation as an Answer to the Problem of Race* (New York: Oxford University Press, 2003), 55.
13. DeYoung, 54.
14. Suetonius, *Divus Claudius* 25.
15. See 1 Corinthians 3:16-17; Ephesians 2:19-22.
16. See Romans 12:4-6.

CHAPTER 6: A HOLE IN OUR DISCIPLESHIP

1. See 1 Peter 2:9.
2. "Grandfather Clause," *Encyclopedia Britannica*, last updated July 22, 2020, https://www.britannica.com/topic/grandfather-clause.
3. Erin Blakemore, "How the GI Bill's Promise Was Denied to a Million Black WWII Veterans," History.com, updated April 20, 2021, https://www.history.com/news/gi-bill-black-wwii-veterans-benefits.
4. I will address the systemic racial injustice that is baked into existing structures that govern American society in chapters 7 and 8.
5. Mark DeYmaz summarizes the findings of Michael O. Emerson and Christian Smith in their 2000 book *Divided by Faith*. See Mark DeYmaz, "Should Pastors Accept or Reject the HUP?," *MarkDeYmaz.com* (blog),

August 25, 2011, https://www.markdeymaz.com/glue/2011/08/should-pastors-accept-or-reject-the-hup.html.

6. See Acts 17:26.

7. Becky Sullivan, "Three Black Soccer Players Are Facing Racist Abuse after England's Euro 2020 Defeat," NPR, updated July 12, 2021, https://www.npr.org/2021/07/12/1015239599/prince-william-and-boris-johnson-denounce-the-racist-abuse-of-englands-soccer-te.

8. See Revelation 7:9.

9. See 2 Corinthians 5:14-20.

10. See Galatians 3:29; 4:19.

11. See 1 John 3:16.

12. See Ephesians 2:14-16; 3:6, 10-11.

13. See 1 John 3:10; John 13:34-35.

14. John M. Perkins, *One Blood: Parting Words to the Church on Race and Love* (Chicago: Moody, 2018), 17.

15. Soong-Chan Rah, *The Next Evangelicalism: Freeing the Church from Western Cultural Captivity* (Downers Grove, IL: IVP Books, 2009), 29–30.

16. See Ephesians 4:16; Romans 12:1-2, 9-21.

17. Matthew J. Hall in Justin Taylor, "A Conversation with Four Historians on the Response of White Evangelicals to the Civil Rights Movement," *Evangelical History* (blog), The Gospel Coalition, July 1, 2016, https://www.thegospel coalition.org/blogs/evangelical-history/a-conversation-with-four-historians-on-the-response-of-white-evangelicals-to-the-civil-rights-movement/.

18. Carolyn Renée Dupont in Justin Taylor, "A Conversation with Four Historians."

19. Derwin L. Gray (@DerwinLGray), Twitter, June 3, 2021, 8:44 a.m., https://twitter.com/DerwinLGray/status/1400448348860162049.

20. Philip Bump, "FBI Director Wray Reconfirms the Threat Posed by Racist Extremists," *Washington Post*, March 2, 2021, https://www.washingtonpost.com/politics/2021/03/02/fbi-director-wray-reconfirms-threat-posed-by-racist-extremists/.

21. Kimmy Yam, "There Were 3,800 Anti-Asian Racist Incidents, Mostly against Women, in Past Year," NBC News, March 16, 2021, https://www.nbcnews.com/news/asian-america/there-were-3-800-anti-asian-racist-incidents-mostly-against-n1261257.

CHAPTER 7: TRUST THE SUPREMACY OF CHRIST

1. Chris Simkins, "Non-violence Was Key to Civil Rights Movement," Voice of America, January 20, 2014, https://www.voanews.com/a/nonviolencekey-to-civil-rights-movement/1737280.html.

2. Dennis R. Edwards, "The Bible in the Civil Rights Movement," Bible Odyssey, accessed March 9, 2021, https://www.bibleodyssey.org/passages /related-articles/bible-in-the-civil-rights-movement.

3. Korie Little Edwards, "The Multiethnic Church Movement Hasn't Lived Up to Its Promise," *Christianity Today*, February 16, 2021, https://www .christianitytoday.com/ct/2021/march/race-diversity-multiethnic-church -movement-promise.html.

4. Martin Luther King Jr., "Dr. Martin Luther King Jr. 1963 WMU Speech Found," Western Michigan University Archives and Regional History Collections and University Libraries, accessed August 20, 2021, https:// wmich.edu/sites/default/files/attachments/MLK.pdf.

5. See Romans 8:11; Revelation 21:1-4; Colossians 3:3-4.

6. See Colossians 1:27-29.

7. John Stott, "The Lausanne Covenant," Lausanne Movement, accessed May 2, 2021, https://lausanne.org/content/covenant/lausanne-covenant#cov.

8. See Galatians 3:8, 28-29.

9. See John 1:14; Romans 5:17.

10. See Colossians 2:14-15.

11. See Matthew 1:23; Hebrews 4:15.

12. John J. Collins and Daniel C. Harlow, eds., *The Eerdmans Dictionary of Early Judaism* (Grand Rapids, MI: Eerdmans, 2010), 671.

13. See Ephesians 2:18-19.

14. See Colossians 3:11.

15. I heard Pastor Miles McPherson give this illustration at the Mosaix National Multiethnic Church Conference in 2016.

16. Jemar Tisby, *How to Fight Racism: Courageous Christianity and the Journey toward Racial Justice* (Grand Rapids, MI: Zondervan Reflective, 2021), 22.

17. Richard Rothstein, *The Color of Law: A Forgotten History of How Our Government Segregated America* (New York: Liveright, 2017), xii.

18. "Athanasius: Five-Time Exile for Fighting 'Orthodoxy,'" *Christianity Today*, accessed August 20, 2021, https://www.christianitytoday.com/history /people/theologians/athanasius.html.

19. Matthew Emerson, "What Do We Do with Karl Barth?," Mere Orthodoxy, October 17, 2017, https://mereorthodoxy.com/what-do-we-do-with-karl -barth/.

20. Robert P. Jones, "Southern Baptists Head for Annual Meeting at a Crossroads on Race and Gender," Religion News Service, June 4, 2021, https://religionnews.com/2021/06/04/southern-baptists-head-for-annual -meeting-at-a-crossroads-on-race-and-gender. For more on the study, see PRRI, https://www.prri.org/research/racial-justice-2020-george-floyd/.

21. Joseph Choi, "Rep. Phillips Says He Did Not Truly Understand White Privilege until the Capitol Riot," *The Hill*, February 4, 2021, https:// thehill.com/homenews/house/537472-rep-phillips-says-he-did-not-truly -understand-privilege-until-the-capitol-riot.

CHAPTER 8: ENGAGE IN DIFFICULT CONVERSATIONS

1. "The Reason Why America Burned Spurgeon's Sermons and Sought to Kill Him," The Spurgeon Center, September 22, 2016, https://www .spurgeon.org/resource-library/blog-entries/the-reason-why-america -burned-spurgeons-sermons-and-sought-to-kill-him/.
2. "Frederick Douglass," *This Far by Faith*, People of Faith, PBS, accessed August 2, 2021, https://www.pbs.org/thisfarbyfaith/people/frederick _douglass.html.
3. Frederick Douglass, quoted at Casey McCorry, "The Pure, Peaceable, Impartial Christianity of Christ," *National Catholic Reporter*, August 5, 2010, https://www.ncronline.org/blogs/ncr-today/pure-peaceable-impartial -christianity-christ.
4. Robert P. Jones, *The End of White Christian America* (New York: Simon & Schuster, 2017), 168.
5. H. Richard Niebuhr, *The Social Sources of Denominationalism* (Gloucester, MA: Peter Smith, 1987), 1029, 239, quoted in Jones, *End of White Christian America*, 164, 166.
6. George Yancey, *Beyond Racial Gridlock: Embracing Mutual Responsibility* (Downers Grove, IL: IVP Books, 2006), 89–90.
7. J. R. R. Tolkien, *The Return of the King* (New York: Del Rey, 2003), 246.
8. Kerr Putney, "A Conversation on Race & Policing," interview by Derwin L. Gray (@derwinlgray), Instagram video, 25:59, May 29, 2020, https://www .instagram.com/tv/CAxrK4hJzLj/?igshid=r7owgy67k14l.
9. See Genesis 1:31; 3:14-24. See also Romans 8:18-39.
10. Anthony Bradley, "Critical Race Theory Isn't a Threat for Presbyterians," Mere Orthodoxy, February 3, 2021, https://mereorthodoxy.com/critical -race-theory-presbyterian-church-in-america/.
11. See 2 Corinthians 5:14-15, 18.

CHAPTER 9: COLLECTIVELY MOURN INJUSTICE

1. Martin Luther King Jr., "Letter from a Birmingham Jail," April 16, 1963, African Studies Center, University of Pennsylvania, https://www.africa .upenn.edu/Articles_Gen/Letter_Birmingham.html.
2. Tony Evans, *Oneness Embraced: Reconciliation, the Kingdom, and How We Are Stronger Together* (Chicago: Moody, 2011), 48.

3. Bridget J. Goosby and Chelsea Heidbrink, "Transgenerational Consequences of Racial Discrimination for African American Health," *Sociology Compass* 7, no. 8 (August 1, 2013): 630–43, https://www.ncbi.nlm.nih.gov/pmc/articles /PMC4026365.
4. Goosby and Heidbrink, "Transgenerational Consequences."
5. See 2 Corinthians 5:20.
6. John Stott, *Christian Mission in the Modern World* (Downers Grove, IL: IVP Books, 2008), 47.
7. Robert P. Jones, *The End of White Christian America* (New York: Simon & Schuster, 2017), 160.
8. Jones, 160.
9. See my book *Building a Multiethnic Church: A Gospel Vision of Love, Grace, and Reconciliation in a Divided World* (Nashville, TN: Thomas Nelson, 2021).
10. Jennifer Harvey, *Dear White Christians: For Those Still Longing for Racial Reconciliation* (Grand Rapids, MI: Eerdmans, 2014), 78–79.

CHAPTER 10: DISPLAY GOSPEL CHARACTER
1. See Colossians 1:24-27.
2. Cathy Lynn Grossman, "U.S. Churchgoers Still Sit in Segregated Pews, and Most Are OK with That," Religion News Service, January 16, 2015, https://religionnews.com/2015/01/16/u-s-churchgoers-still-sit-segregated -pews-ok/.
3. Bob Smietana, "Sunday Morning Segregation: Most Worshipers Feel Their Church Has Enough Diversity," *Christianity Today*, January 15, 2015, https://www.christianitytoday.com/news/2015/january/sunday-morning -segregation-most-worshipers-church-diversity.html.
4. Mark DeYmaz, "Ethnic Blends: Growing Healthy, Multiethnic Churches," Lifeway Research, October 9, 2014, https://lifewayresearch.com/2014 /10/09/ethnic-blends-growing-healthy-multiethnic-churches/.
5. Michael O. Emerson, "A New Day for Multiracial Congregations," *Reflections*, Spring 2013, https://reflections.yale.edu/article/future-race /new-day-multiracial-congregations.
6. N. T. Wright, "What Is the Point of Celebrating Easter during a Pandemic?," *Time*, April 2, 2021, https://time.com/5951865/celebrating-easter-during -a-pandemic/.
7. See Ephesians 2:14-16; Romans 8:29.
8. "Ephesians: The Third Race (2:11-18)," Truth for Today, accessed August 24, 2021, http://biblecourses.com/English/en_lessons/EN_199502_11.pdf.
9. See Ephesians 2:1-3.
10. See Ephesians 2:4-7.

11. Jesus most likely also tore the veil in the Holy of Holies. See Matthew 27:51.
12. Bob Utley, *Paul Bound, the Gospel Unbound: Letters from Prison (Colossians, Ephesians, Philemon then later, Philippians)* (Marshall, TX: Bible Lessons International, 1997), Ephesians 2:14.

CHAPTER 11: AFFIRM THE RECONCILER'S CREED

1. Greg Fromholz, "Redemption—The John M. Perkins Story," YouTube video, 21:04, May 17, 2018, https://www.youtube.com/watch?v=scRpgoR_qyo.
2. This was a conversation that Dr. Perkins, my son, my wife, and I had over dinner at a restaurant in Charlotte, North Carolina.
3. John M. Perkins, *One Blood: Parting Words to the Church on Race and Love* (Chicago: Moody, 2018), 32, 39.
4. See Colossians 3:1-11; Romans 12:1-2.
5. See Psalm 96.
6. See Mark 12:29-31.
7. See Romans 12:1.
8. See Ephesians 1:3.
9. See Romans 5:12-20.
10. A. W. Tozer, *The Knowledge of the Holy: The Attributes of God: Their Meaning in the Christian Life* (San Francisco: HarperSanFrancisco, 1992), 165–66.
11. See my book *The Good Life: What Jesus Teaches about Finding True Happiness* (Nashville, TN: B&H, 2020).
12. See Colossians 3:8-9.
13. See Ephesians 1:4.
14. See Luke 9:35.
15. Soong-Chan Rah, *The Next Evangelicalism: Freeing the Church from Western Cultural Captivity* (Downers Grove: IVP Books, 2009), 29.
16. Quina Aragon, "What Do You Mean by 'Unity'?," The Gospel Coalition, January 18, 2021, https://www.thegospelcoalition.org/article/what-you-mean-unity/.
17. See Ephesians 1:4, 7, 13-14.
18. See Romans 6:4.
19. See Romans 4:16-17.
20. See 1 John 4:9-11.

CONCLUSION: PASSING THE TORCH

1. Atlanta Committee for the Olympic Games, "1936–1992: History of Olympic Torch Relays," *Washington Post*, accessed May 8, 2021, https://www.washingtonpost.com/wp-srv/sports/olympics/longterm/torches/history.htm.

About the Author

DR. DERWIN L. GRAY is the cofounder and lead pastor of Transformation Church (TC), a multiethnic, multigenerational, mission-shaped church located in the metro region of Charlotte, North Carolina. He is a popular conference speaker and the author of *Hero: Unleashing God's Power in a Man's Heart, Building a Multiethnic Church, The Good Life, Limitless Life,* and *God, Do You Hear Me?* Derwin earned a master of divinity with a concentration in apologetics from Southern Evangelical Seminary under the mentorship of the renowned theologian Dr. Norman Geisler. He also earned a doctor of ministry in the New Testament in context at Northern Seminary under Scot McKnight. Derwin met his wife, Vicki, at Brigham Young University, and they have been married since 1992. They have two adult children, Presley and Jeremiah.

TRANSFORMATION
C H U R C H

Dr. Derwin L. Gray is the lead pastor and cofounder (along with his wife, Vicki) of Transformation Church (TC) in Indian Land, South Carolina.

Pastor Derwin has a passion for bringing together people who are devoted to loving God completely, loving themselves correctly, and loving their neighbors compassionately.

If you are looking for a church community that is
• multiethnic • multigenerational • mission-shaped
then TC is the church for you!

In addition to his role at Transformation Church,
Pastor Derwin speaks at churches and conferences nationwide.

For more information about Pastor Derwin's speaking
opportunities, visit derwinlgray.com/teaching-engagement.
For more information about Transformation Church, visit transformationchurch.tc.

CP1770